STAND-

by Bill Cain

with music by Craig Sibley

SAMUEL FRENCH, INC.

45 West 25th Street   NEW YORK 10010
7623 Sunset Boulevard HOLLYWOOD 90046
LONDON   TORONTO

Stand-Up Tragedy is dedicated to
Tom G.—Jairo—Kevin.
The students and faculty of
Nativity Mission School.
The 17th Street Jesuit (and beyond)
Community.
Everyone at the Mark Taper Forum.
and
Wade Pizarro—the creator of "Saga"

Samuel French, Inc. can supply amateurs with a cassette of the RAP MUSIC actually used in the New York production, as composed by Craig Sibley, upon receipt of the following:

$32.50 purchase price;

A music royalty fee of $10 for each performance for the entire run;

$2.50 to cover postage and handling; and

The number of performances and exact performance dates.

In addition to the above please note that once an order for a tape is filled and in the mail, the music royalty is not refundable.

Stock royalty terms upon application.

IMPORTANT BILLING AND CREDIT
REQUIREMENTS

All producers of STAND-UP TRAGEDY *must* give credit to the Author of the Play in all programs distributed in connection with performances of the Play and in all instances in which the title of the Play appears for purposes of advertising, publicizing or otherwise exploiting the Play and/or a production. The name of the Author *must* also appear on a separate line, on which no other name appears, immediately following the title, and *must* appear in size of type not less than fifty percent the size of the title type.

After being workshopped in the New Works Festival '88 and then presented as a Taper, Too production, *Stand-Up Tragedy* was presented on the main stage of the Mark Taper Forum in Los Angeles (Gordon Davidson, Artistic Director; Stephen J. Albert, Managing Director; Robert Egan, Associate Artistic Director) on May 20, 1989. The production was directed by Ron Link; set designed by Yael Pardess; costumes designed by Carol Brolaski; lighting designed by Michael Gilliam; sound designed by Jon Gottlieb; original music composed by Craig Sibley; rap choreography by Shabba-Doo; associate producer—Corey Beth Madden; production supervisors—Robert Routolo and Frank Bayer; production stage manager—Mary Michele Miner; stage manager—Cari Norton. The cast (in alphabetical order) was as follows:

Fr. Ed Larkin	Vaughn Armstrong
Marco Ruiz	Anthony Barrile
Freddy	Marcus Chong
Tom Griffin	Jack Coleman
Luis	Marvin Columbus
Mitchell James	John C. Cooke
Lee Cortez	Michael DeLorenzo
Burke Kendall	Dan Gerrity
Henry Rodriguez	Ray Oriel
Carlos	Lance Slaughter

On October 4, 1990, Charles B. Moss, Jr., Brent Peek and Donald Taffner Presented The Center Theatre Group/Mark Taper Forum and Hartford Stage Company (Mark Lamos, Artistic Director; David Hawkanson, Managing Director) Production of *Stand-Up Tragedy* on Broadway at the Criterion Center, Stage Right. The production was directed by Ron Link; set designed by Yael Pardess; costumes designed by Carol Brolaski; lighting designed by Michael Gilliam; sound design by Jon Gottlieb; original music by Craig Sibley; casting by Johnson-Liff & Zerman; rap choreograph by Charles Randolph-Wright; production stage manager – Franklin Keysar; production supervisor – Frank Bayer; stage manager – Ruth E. Sternberg; dramaturg – Corey Beth Madden. The cast (in alphabetical order) was as follows:

Marco Ruiz	Anthony Barrile
Lee Cortez	Marcus Chong
Fr. Ed Larkin	Charles Cioffi
Tom Griffin	Jack Coleman
Mitchell James	John C. Cooke
Freddy	Robert Barry Fleming
Burke Kendall	Dan Gerrity
Carlos	Darrin DeWitt Henson
Henry Rodriguez	Ray Oriel

Standbys:
For the faculty—Christopher Cass; for Lee and Marco—Robert Barry Fleming; for Henry—Darrin DeWitt Henson; for Carlos and Freddy—Marc Joseph.

CHARACTERS

STUDENTS:

LEE CORTEZ – 14 years old. Puerto Rican. Withdrawn. Very thin. Worlds inside.

HENRY RODRIGUEZ – Dominican. Fleshy and flashy.

OTHERS: FREDDY, MARCO, CARLOS – Should fit into a Hispanic junior high school.

TEACHERS:

FR. ED LARKIN – Catholic priest. Jesuit. Principal. A jock and a drill sergeant.

TOM GRIFFIN – Right out of college. A straight arrow. A wicked tongue and relentless sense of humor. An athlete of body and spirit. Gets what he wants.

BURKE KENDALL – Been teaching for years. Goes to the opera as often as possible.

MITCHELL JAMES – Four years at the school. About to become a fixture. Thinks of himself as an expert on discipline because he has to spend so much time fighting for it.

(We will also meet Lee's family in the monologues: his mother, his older brother Tyro, his younger brother and sister, and Tyro's girl friend, Maritza.)

PLACE

In and around a small Catholic school for Hispanic boys on the Lower East Side of Manhattan.

The apartments of the boys and the teachers.

The streets.

Places inside their minds.

There must be no attempt to make realistic sets or props. Light and sound suggestions only, please.

ACT I: First semester.

ACT II: Second semester.

(Further notes on production follow the text.)

A Note on Stand-Up Tragedy

It's stand-up comedy inside out.

As a stand-up comic will become—unannounced—other characters in his or her life, so too will a stand-up tragedian.

This will feel chaotic at the start. I thought of cleaning it up with notes, but decided against it. It should feel chaotic. It's chaos.

The monologues should use all the energy, humor, and inventiveness that a modern stand-up comic would bring to his or her work.

On a number of occasions, characters speak their thoughts rather than their lines. Again, I've used no notes to indicate this. I hope it's clear from the text.

As for the basketball games, the raps, the one-character fist fights et al. . . . good luck.

One other thought—As the characters' problems become more serious, please don't lose your sense of humor.

There is always a sense of absurdity even at the most critical moments on the Lower East Side.

Bill Cain

ACT I

Scene 1

Two loud SHOTS.
A funeral. A wide purple stole over his shoulders,
LARKIN enters, followed by a STUDENT who carries
a liturgical pail which contains holy water and a
sprinkler.

LARKIN. (*Darkly amused.*) I've learned to tell who's
new to the neighborhood by how high they jump when a
gun goes off. There are always shots in this neighborhood.
You get used to them. Just like there are always funerals.
(*LARKIN sprinkles water on the audience.*) May the angels
lead you into paradise . . . (*LARKIN places sprinkler into
pail.*) This school is filled with kids who have dead older
brothers. I said most of their funerals. I was inspiring. I
taught them math, diagramming sentences . . . and then I
prayed that the angels would lead them into paradise.
(*Retrieving sprinkler.*) I think I want to start a *new*
religion—one that doesn't think that angels are going to
lead anybody anywhere . . . (*Water to the right . . .*) . . .
one that doesn't pretend that the poor are blessed . . .
(*Water to the left . . .*) . . . one that doesn't use a dead
young man as its logo. (*Water center.*) Forgive me, but
after last year it's a little hard to be inspiring. I suppose I
should be thanking you all for coming to his funeral, but
there's this question that keeps going around in my mind .

11

. . (*After a pause:*) Where the fuck were you when he was dying?

(*Pause—then insistent school BELL.*)

ACT I

Scene 2

LARKIN holds his ground as the school explodes around him. The TEACHERS and the STUDENTS of Trinity Mission School end up in formal positions for assembly. LARKIN addresses them as if they were a larger group.

KENDALL. Gentlemen, the National Anthem.
ALL. (*Singing out beautifully.*) Oh, say can you see! And the home of the brave!
LARKIN. In the name of the . . .
ALL. Father, Son, Holy Spirit.
LARKIN. Prayer.
ALL. Father, Son, Holy Spirit. Amen.

(*STUDENTS kiss their hands on the amen.*)

LARKIN. (*Towards audience.*) Gentlemen—teachers and students—welcome back to Trinity Mission School. Almost all of you have made it back. Except. Except the few who chose the streets. Like Ramon Cruz. If any of you want to see what Ramon is up to, all you have to do is look out those windows . . .

(STUDENTS look toward windows.)

LARKIN. He'll be selling in the park every day now. Any of you care to join him? No? Good! You are *different*. You are taking responsibility for your lives. You know what that means—responsibility?

(Strong SPOTLIGHT on LARKIN. Although Larkin's speech is compressed in form, it is passionate, sincere and spirited.)

LARKIN. Definition of responsibility. Webster's definition. My personal definition. Anecdote about responsibility. Joke about last year's graduating class.

(Laughter from the STUDENTS.)

LARKIN. Small joke about myself to balance it off.

(Laughter from STUDENTS and TEACHERS.)

LARKIN. Anecdote about a former student. And you know what that boy is today? Pause for effect. He's a lawyer! Or—he's a convicted felon . . . depending on the nature of the anecdote. *Metaphor. Good* metaphor. *Unembarrassed* metaphor. Stars! Mountains! *Goals!* Beethoven wrote the Ninth Symphony deaf! Homer wrote the Odyssey blind! One-legged pole vaulters! Organ donors!

Christ himself! Building now. High hopes! High expectations! God's blessing! FIRST SEMESTER!

(School BELL. Instantly the assembly becomes a classroom.)

JAMES. OK, gentlemen—take out your notebooks.
KENDALL. I want you to get all of this down.
LARKIN. *Of course* neatness counts and—yes—
TEACHERS. IT *WILL* BE ON THE TEST! *EVERYTHING* WILL *ALWAYS* BE *ON THE TEST!* OK?
STUDENTS. OK!
TEACHERS. O*K*!
KENDALL. We will begin with . . .
TEACHERS. HISTORY!

(School BELL.)

KENDALL. Here we go!
JAMES. *(Rapid fire.)* The dinosaurs . . .
LARKIN. *(Rapid fire.)* The Greeks . . .
KENDALL. *(Rapid fire.)* The Romans . . .
LARKIN. The Dark Ages . . .
JAMES. The Renaissance . . .
LARKIN. Napoleon . . .
JAMES. Kennedy . . .
KENDALL. The Vietnam War . . .
KENDALL. *(After brief pause.)* . . . and that's pretty much history.

(School BELL. STUDENTS and TEACHERS change classes. KENDALL and JAMES exit. STUDENTS regroup to become Larkin's class.)

LARKIN. (*Rapid fire.*) OK, take out your math books. Review, review, review.

STUDENTS. (*Spirited.*) Review, review, review.

LARKIN. Yada, yada, yada.

STUDENTS. Yada, yada, yada.

LARKIN. Addition.

MARCO. Subtraction.

LARKIN. Multiplication.

CARLOS. Division.

LARKIN. OK. New work. Word problems. Now the key to word problems is understanding the words, OK?

STUDENTS. OK.

LARKIN. O*K*. So, take the first one, Marco. Page 6, bottom of the page.

MARCO. (*Leaping to his feet.*) If a student is mowing his neighbor's lawn for $3 a square yard . . .

LARKIN. Anybody here have a neighbor with a lawn? . . . No? OK.

STUDENTS. OK.

LARKIN. O*K*, let's try a different one. Carlos, problem set, page 9, top of the page, please . . .

CARLOS. (*To his feet.*) If a man is chopping wood for this fireplace at the rate of one ten-foot tree every twenty minutes . . .

LARKIN. OK. Anybody here got a fireplace? . . . No? OK.

STUDENTS. OK.

LARKIN. O*K*, let's move along. Page 15, middle of the page, Lee. (*No response.*) Lee . . . Lee! . . . Lidelfo, where's your book? (*No response.*) Lee, stand up. Lee, where's your book?

(*LEE is very self-conscious. HE is unprepared, distracted and tired.*)

LEE. (*Inward.*) I forgot it.
LARKIN. You "forgot it"?
LEE. Yes.
LARKIN. Yes, what?
LEE. *Yes, Your Holiness.*
LARKIN. Yes, *Father Larkin*. That's better. You "forgot" the book. That's a second grade sort of excuse for an eighth grader to be using, isn't it?
LEE. Yes.
LARKIN. Yes, what?
LEE. *Yes, Your Whiteness.*
LARKIN. Yes, *Father Larkin*. That's better. "Forgot?" I mean, really, Lee. After all summer long to come up with excuses, you forgot? How about: "I started out with all of my books this morning, Father, but on the way to school a group of Trinity dropouts mugged me saying, "We don't care about your money, but *please* you *must* give me your Algebra I text."
LEE. (*After a brief pause.*) Yeah, that's what happened to me. (*LEE starts to sit.*)
LARKIN. (*Gesturing for him to rise.*) Nonononono. You have to come up with an excuse of your own.
LEE. (*At a loss.*) I forgot it.
LARKIN. Take jug this afternoon, Lee.

(Groans and laughter from the STUDENTS.)

LARKIN. You still want to go to Art and Design next year, Lee?

LEE. Yes.

LARKIN. Well, you're not going to make it this way, boy. Better wake up and smell the coffee, Lee. Take a seat.

(LEE remains standing. LARKIN continues to teach math silently.)

LEE. I had things on my mind, Father Larkin. (*Loud sound of BREAKING GLASS. Strong SPOTLIGHT on LEE as HE enters his own world. With great violence:*) SHIT! I CUT MY FUCKING HAND. NOW SEE WHAT YOU MADE ME DO! Wrap it up like this. THE FUCKING TOWEL IS FILTHY! You're getting it on my books. I'M FUCKING BLEEDING AND YOU'RE WORRIED ABOUT YOUR BOOKS! You're scaring the kids. ARE YOU SCARED? No, Tyro. SO DON'T TALK ABOUT WHAT YOU DON'T KNOW ABOUT. GET SOMETHING TO CLEAN ME UP. I gave you the towel. I don't want the towel. THEN WHAT THE FUCK DO YOU WANT?

KENDALL. (*Appearing—return to the classroom.*) I want you to tell me what an interrogative sentence is. *Lee!* Is there anybody in there, Lee? Are you awake, Lee?

LEE. (*As Señora..*) Yes, I'm awake. How do you expect me to sleep with the two of you making all that noise?

KENDALL. I hope I haven't disturbed your nap, Lee. Can I get you anything—a cup of coffee, perhaps?

LARKIN. (*Señora.*) A cup of coffee would be nice. Get me my cigarettes too, OK?

KENDALL. Types of sentences, Lee. Now make me a happy man and tell me you remember some of this from last year.

LEE. (*Señora.*) Yes, I remember. I left them on the table.

KENDALL. Good. Then give me an example of an interrogative sentence.

LEE. (*Señora.*) What do you mean they're not there?

KENDALL. Good. Declarative.

LEE. (*Señora.*) There were cigarettes there when I went to bed.

KENDALL. Imperative.

LEE. (*Señora.*) Give me some of yours!

KENDALL. Exclamatory.

LEE. (*Señora.*) No! No?!? So you think you the big man! Who the fuck are you to tell me *No*!?!

KENDALL. Good, Good, good, good. It's good to see at least one of you has remembered something from last year. Thank you, Lee. You can take a seat. Lee? Lee, take a seat unless there's something you want to ask.

(Slam! SPOTLIGHT on LEE.)

LEE. (*With increasing violence.*)YEAH, I GOT A QUESTION. I NEED SOME MONEY TO GO OUT WITH MARITZA. Look in my purse—you can take what's there. THERE'S NOTHING THERE. Yeah, and that's what you can have. THE CHECK CAME TODAY. The check's not for you; it's for the kids. I'M ONE OF THE KIDS. Not anymore. YOU TOOK ME OFF? The

lady took you off cause you're not in school anymore. I
NEED THE MONEY. I need the money too. I got a rash
on my arms and welfare don't pay for Dove soap. YOU
HAD ENOUGH MONEY TO GET DRUNK! NEVER,
NEVER CALL YOUR MOTHER DRUNK, EVEN IF
SHE IS. RESPETO! HAND! SLAP! FIST! FIST! FIST!
LEE! LEE! LEE! GET YOUR BROTHER OFF ME, LEE!

    ALL. (*Creating the world of SAGA.*) SA – GA! SA –
GA! SA – GA!

    LEE. *I challenge you to single combat!*
    STUDENTS. SA – GA! SA – GA! SA – GA!
    LEE. *The choice of the weapons is yours . . .*
    STUDENTS. FIGHT!
    LEE. YES! TO THE DEATH?
    STUDENTS. YES!
    LEE. KILL?
    STUDENTS. YES!
    LEE. KILL!
    STUDENTS. YES!
    LEE. KILL!
    STUDENTS. YES!

(*GRIFFIN, cheerfully unaware of the chaos around him,
    replaces LEE in the center of the shouting students.*)

    GRIFFIN. *Teacher!*
    STUDENTS. Yes!
    GRIFFIN. *Responsible!*
    STUDENTS. Yes!
    GRIFFIN. *Inspiring!*
    STUDENTS. NO!
    GRIFFIN. *Role Model!*

STUDENTS. WHITE BOY!
GRIFFIN. *Einstein!*
STUDENTS. EWING!
GRIFFIN. *Mozart!*
STUDENTS. MAGIC!
GRIFFIN. *Jesus!*
STUDENTS. JORDAN!
GRIFFIN. *You too can be an overachiever! Right?*
STUDENTS. WRONG!
GRIFFIN. Good! Good work. End of pep talk. Back to lesson!

(ALL STUDENTS but LEE sit and return to classroom mode. LEE remains standing in his private world.)

LEE. . . . but no one took Saga's challenge, for they knew his reputation in war and they backed off in fear and bowed to him. (*LEE waves his arm to acknowledge the crowd's ROAR.*)
GRIFFIN. (*Noticing Lee's hand in the air.*) Yes? Hey. Hey. *LEE!*

(LEE wakes up.)

GRIFFIN. You got a question?
LEE. No.
GRIFFIN. Then what's your hand doing in the air?

(STUDENTS react. LEE pulls hand down.)

GRIFFIN. Say, where were you, boy?
LEE. Here.

GRIFFIN. No, I mean, where were you *really*? In bed with some slick chick?

LEE. *STAY OUT OF MY MIND!*

GRIFFIN. Excuse me. I can't hear you.

LEE. Nothing.

GRIFFIN. Was it sexual, fantasy, señor?

(LEE reacts.)

GRIFFIN. Woooo, it was, wasn't it?

(Major STUDENT response.)

GRIFFIN. OK, Lee, I'm reviewing this for you, so pay special attention, OK? Lee? LEE!

LEE. OK.

GRIFFIN. What's the most important date in modern times?

CARLOS. The day they dropped the atom bomb?

GRIFFIN. No.

FREDDY. When they ended the Viet Nam War?

GRIFFIN. No.

HENRY. The day Patrick Ewing joined the Knicks?

GRIFFIN. No, but you're getting close.

LEE. The day you were born?

GRIFFIN. Good. *VERY* good—the day I was born. And how do we *know* that's the most important date in modern times.

MARCO. Because you're a new teacher and all new teachers think they're the center of the world.

GRIFFIN. Excellent! And what's the most important decision ever made?

CARLOS. Your decision to teach here?

GRIFFIN. Excellent! Excellent! Good class! Would you like to hear about it?

STUDENTS. *NO!*

(Slam! GRIFFIN in a SPOTLIGHT addresses the audience.)

GRIFFIN. (*Immediately.*) Well, it was a hard decision—lots of parental expectations to let down—but, face it, all the best minds of my generation are going into marketing for Hormel—or doing bond issues for Smith Barney—which is basically the same thing only at least with Hormel you can eat the baloney, right? And for what? *What good* are they ever going to do anybody but themselves? And they say it's just a first job; it's not a life and death decision. But, see, what they don't know is—that *every* decision . . . is a life and death decision. So why did I come here?

STUDENTS. Because you're such a good guy?

GRIFFIN. (*Back to the classroom.*) Exactly! I'm such a good guy!

(Noticing LEE again in a different world.)

GRIFFIN. And that's why it pisses me off when—while I'm trying to introduce you to the crucial turning points in Western Civilization—some kid chooses to *doodle.* (*Tearing a page out of Lee's book.*) Very disappointing. Not even pornographic. Stand up, Lee.

(LEE stands.)

GRIFFIN. Quick quiz—what is the pivotal event in the history of the modern world?

LEE. The day Saga was born . . .

GRIFFIN. And what's the date on that?

LEE. No date. Saga was born before time . . .

GRIFFIN. And where was he born?

LEE. In my eyes.

GRIFFIN. Hey, hey, hey—you're missing the main event here, boy. Did you even get my name?

HENRY. I know it.

GRIFFIN. (*To Lee.*) Lee, say my name.

LEE. I don't know it.

GRIFFIN. The body and the hind legs of a lion and the head and wings of an eagle.

LEE. A griffin.

(*STUDENTS applaud.*)

GRIFFIN. (*Writing his name on the board.*) They told me you were the school expert on mythology. My name is *Tom* Griffin.

LEE. (*Shouting.*) *I DON'T WANT TO KNOW YOUR FIRST NAME!*

GRIFFIN. Now you might not want to know my first name, but I think if we're going to work together, we should know something about each other. I inherited the name Griffin and it fits me cause I've got the strength of a lion and I can soar like an eagle.

(STUDENTS scream like eagles and follow as LEE leads a ritual hunt for the Griffin. GRIFFIN, unaware, continues to teach.)

LEE. *(Chant/rap.)* CROSS A LION AND AN EAGLE AND IN THE BOOKS I'VE READ . . .

GRIFFIN. *(Checks his watch.)* OK, you got what you wanted, Lee . . .

LEE. . . . YOU GET A LION'S BODY WITH AN EAGLE'S HEAD.

GRIFFIN. I wasted the period.

STUDENTS. All right!

LEE. BUT AFTER ALL THAT TROUBLE YOU GOT TO WONDER WHY . . .

GRIFFIN. But so it won't be a *total* waste . . .

LEE. . . . 'CAUSE IT LOOKS GREAT ON PAPER BUT IT'S NEVER GONNA FLY.

GRIFFIN. . . . . We will preview your biology homework on *blood*!

STUDENTS. NO!

(STUDENTS slowly surround Griffin and close in on him.)

GRIFFIN. YES! Blood *is* thicker than water . . .

LEE. WHEN SAGA PULLED HIS KNIFE THE GRIFFIN SHOULD HAVE KNOWN. . .

GRIFFIN. The heart pumps the blood through the body. . .

LEE. IF THE GRIFFIN WAS SMART, THE GRIFFIN WOULD HAVE FLOWN.

GRIFFIN. . . . *out* through the arteries; *back* through the veins . . .

LEE. WHEN SAGA WAS READY, SAGA WOULD SPRING . . .

GRIFFIN. . . . and keeping that blood going around is our life's main task!

LEE. SAGA'S ONLY WAITING FOR THE SCHOOL BELL TO RING!

(The BELL rings. LEE screams as HE slits Griffin's throat. GRIFFIN screams and screams until the BELL stops ringing. Then, as if nothing had happened:)

GRIFFIN. *(Cheerful.)* OK, *good first day*, everybody!

(Heavy rap BEAT starts immediately. GRIFFIN exits, leaving STUDENTS to create the world of Saga.)

[handwritten margin note: wants to get rid of Griffin hated antagonist]

ACT I

Scene 3

STUDENTS now rap and dance the Saga of SAGA.

LEE. *(Spoken.)*
SAGA WAS BIG. SAGA WAS BUILT.
SAGA HAD TO ANSWER FOR THE BLOOD THAT
   WAS SPILT.
   STUDENTS. *(Rap.)*
SAGA WAS BIG. SAGA WAS TOUGH.

NO PRISON *BUILT BY MAN* COULD BE STRONG
    ENOUGH
TO TIE SAGA DOWN—TO HOLD SAGA BACK.
HE COULD BREAK OUT OF JAIL AND GO ON THE
    ATTACK.
ON THE ATTACK!
NO *MAN'S* PRISON COULD DO SAGA IN . . .
    LEE.
BUT YOUR FAMILY'S A PRISON . . .
    STUDENTS.
. . . *GOD* PUTS YOU IN.
    LEE.
YOUR FAMILY'S A PRISON . . .
    STUDENTS.
. . . *GOD* PUTS YOU IN.

*(During a dance break, LEE redoes his "Shit, I cut my
    fucking hand" stand-up.)*

    MARCO.
SEE GOD IS FUNNY. HE LIKES A GOOD LAUGH—
SO HE MADE SAGA'S FAMILY FOR A LAUGH AND
    A HALF.
SEE, THE BARON'S HIS—
    ALL STUDENTS.
FATHER!
    MARCO.
THE SHADOW'S HIS—
    ALL STUDENTS.
BRO!
    MARCO.
AND WHEN THE BARON MEETS THE SHADOW—

ALL STUDENTS.
THE BLOOD IS GONNA FLOW.
    MARCO.
SEE, IN THE BARON'S CASTLE THERE WAS
    ALWAYS BLOOD.
THEY HAD BLOOD BY THE BARREL—
    ALL STUDENTS.
BLOOD BY THE FLOOD.
    MARCO.
THEY HAD TYPE A—
    FREDDY.
TYPE B—
    HENRY.
AND TYPE O—
    MARCO.
THEY HAD BLOOD ON TAP—
    ALL STUDENTS.
THEY HAD BLOOD—TO—GO.

(A second dance break featuring LEE.)

    ALL STUDENTS.
SAGA WAS BIG. SAGA WAS BUILT.
SAGA HAD TO ANSWER FOR THE BLOOD THAT
    WAS SPILT.
ONE THING SAGA NEVER COULD DECIDE—
    LEE.
WHY WAS IT SO HARD TO KEEP THE BLOOD
    INSIDE?
    ALL STUDENTS.
SEE, THAT WAS HIS JOB. THAT WAS HIS CHORE

*TO STOP ALL THAT BLOOD—WITHOUT SPILLING
    MORE.*

(Third dance break.)

    ALL STUDENTS.
BLOOD!
BY THE FLOOD!
BLOOD!
BY THE FLOOD!
BLOOD!
BY THE FLOOD!
BLOOD!

(School BELL. STUDENTS scatter.)

ACT I

Scene 4

LARKIN addresses the audience.

    LARKIN. Ninety-nine percent of what goes on in *any*
school is *routine*. It's the principal's main job to make
sure that the remaining one percent doesn't blow the whole
place to kingdom come.

*(Short school BELL. LIGHTS change: A teachers'
    meeting.)*

LARKIN. (*Driving.*) Rules for the staff of Trinity Mission School. (This is for the new teacher; the old ones know it by heart.) Rule one:

ALL. (*But GRIFFIN.*) TEACH!

LARKIN. Rule two:

ALL. (*But GRIFFIN.*) TEACH!

LARKIN. Rule three:

ALL. (*But GRIFFIN.*) Teach some more.

LARKIN. Rule four . . .

GRIFFIN. TEACH!

(Annoyed by the interruption, LARKIN and TEACHERS look at Griffin.)

GRIFFIN. Sorry . . . but I was close, wasn't I?

LARKIN. You want to hear these rules or not?

KENDALL. Rule four?

LARKIN. (*Driving on.*) Rule four: Ask for the moon from these kids *and get it*! Rule five: If you can't get it from them, go teach at the public school down the block. The principal there has a sign in his office. It says, "The three best things about teaching are June, July and August." But he's a good man in his own way. He's got a lot of sympathy for these kids since they come from such a deprived neighborhood. He also has reading scores that are through the floor. Which brings me to our final rule. Rule 6: Be callous. So their father's a junkie. So what? So their mother's a slave in some factory. Big deal. They don't need sympathy. They need to learn skills. So *teach, teach,* and *teach some more.*

be rough
pound on
something

(School BELL rings. Exit GRIFFIN and LARKIN. KENDALL and JAMES teach to the audience as if it were a class.)

KENDALL. Aboard, about, above, according to, across, along, by, by way of, by means of . . .

JAMES. Actinium, aluminum, americium, argon, arsenic . . . Over the course of the year we will be learning the names of all the elements . . .

KENDALL. Any student who can name all fifty-three prepositions in less than twenty seconds . . .

JAMES. Any student who fails to learn them . . .

KENDALL. . . . will be given a prize.

JAMES. . . . will have his fingers cut off. No, not actually. Unfortunately, you will merely be suspended. Now . . .

KENDALL. . . . Now let us begin by correcting some popular misconceptions . . .

JAMES. . . . we will begin with the universe . . .

KENDALL. These are called PREPositions, not PROPositions . . .

JAMES. There is no planet Krypton . . .

KENDALL. That little punctuation mark is pronounced apostrophe, not a pastrami . . .

JAMES. At no point in science class will we discuss Klingons . . .

KENDALL. A period comes at the end of a sentence, not at the end of a month . . .

JAMES. . . . and the Big Bang theory is *not* what you think it is.

KENDALL and JAMES. Is that clear?

JAMES. (*Earnest.*) Now, moving along, there are some further questions that I feel we should consider . . .

KENDALL. . . . . at least for those of you who are ready for more advanced work. For example, can any of you tell me why am I working here for nothing when I could be making much more word processing for a temp agency?

(Silence.)

JAMES. No? Well, maybe that's too hard for openers. How about this—can anyone here figure out why I do anything more than go through the motions—when I *know* that most of you are going to drop out by the time you're half way through high school—regardless of what I do?

(Silence.)

KENDALL. And, of course, the ultimate extra credit question . . .

JAMES and KENDALL. Is it too late for me to go to law school?

(School BELL. JAMES and KENDALL exit. STUDENTS fly through the halls.
LARKIN and GRIFFIN pass each other in a corridor.)

LARKIN. Oh, Tom . . .

GRIFFIN. Yes, Father . . .

LARKIN. Maybe I didn't mention this before, but we have mass in the morning here every day.

GRIFFIN. No, you told me.

LARKIN. Oh.

GRIFFIN. (*After brief pause.*) It's not compulsory, is it?

LARKIN. No, it's not compulsory, but the faculty is expected to attend. (*LARKIN starts to exit.*)

GRIFFIN. Hey, hey, hey. That's it? No comment on the class?

LARKIN. I thought you were . . . fine.

GRIFFIN. Fine? What's "fine" around here? a B? a B-? What?

LARKIN. I thought you were fine . . . today.

GRIFFIN. Today?

LARKIN. Over the past week I've had some complaints, but today you were fine so I thought I'd let it go. Unless you think an explanation is in order.

GRIFFIN. Yes, I do.

LARKIN. Well?

GRIFFIN. Well, I think you ought to get the students who complained to explain it to you.

LARKIN. They weren't students.

GRIFFIN. (*After brief pause.*) Oh.

LARKIN. It's a small school, Tom. Word gets around.

GRIFFIN. I see. (*GRIFFIN starts to exit.*)

LARKIN. Tom . . .

(*GRIFFIN stops.*)

LARKIN. Tom, did you call Jesus an overachiever?

GRIFFIN. (*After a brief pause.*) Well, Father, the guy rose from the dead. I'd call that overachieving, wouldn't you?

(*No response from LARKIN. Awkward silence.*)

GRIFFIN. Anything else?

LARKIN. (*New level of seriousness.*) Yes. I hear you were being kind of rough on Lee Cortez.

GRIFFIN. I thought we weren't supposed to have sympathy. Just following instructions, Father.

LARKIN. My instructions weren't meant as a license to attack students. The kids need to be inspired.

GRIFFIN. So inspire them . . .

LARKIN. Yes . . .

GRIFFIN. . . . like you did at the opening assembly— threatening them with failing out?

LARKIN. Well, some of them are. That's just the way it is. Not even Jesus could save them all. You think you can improve on his percentages?

GRIFFIN. (*Delighting in this.*) I can try. There was this medieval saint—you may not have heard of him—he never made it into the Church canon for obvious reasons— see, he *earned* heaven but when he got to the gates, he wouldn't go in.

LARKIN. No?

GRIFFIN. No—not unless they'd empty hell and let *everybody* in with him.

LARKIN. So that's what Georgetown is teaching in Trendy Theology 101 these days?

GRIFFIN. (*New level of seriousness.*) It was a 400 course in City Planning. You can't save *some* of a city.

LARKIN. (*Enough crap, to the bone.*) You hurt him.

GRIFFIN. I beg your pardon?

LARKIN. Lee—you hurt him.

GRIFFIN. He told you that?

LARKIN. He doesn't tell anybody much of anything, does he?

GRIFFIN. Then how . . .

LARKIN. Like I said, word gets around. A little courtesy would go a long way.

GRIFFIN. (*Knee jerk.*) Yeah, how far has it gone with him so far?

(*LARKIN, offended, starts to exit.*)

GRIFFIN. Wait. What . . . (*Enough crap. To the bone.*) What should I do?

LARKIN. (*After a brief pause.*) Nothing.

GRIFFIN. Nothing?

LARKIN. Nothing. Sometimes that's best.

GRIFFIN. I'm afraid I've never been very good at that.

LARKIN. Why not?

GRIFFIN. (*Honest.*) Well, Father, I guess it has to do with *my* personal definition of responsibility.

(*School BELL.*)

ACT I

Scene 5

A classroom.

KENDALL is teachng a full class, but we see only HENRY. Other STUDENTS comment from casual positions around the set.

KENDALL. Henry, you haven't done one homework assignment in the month since school started. Would you be so kind as to tell me *why*?

HENRY. I don't want to.

(STUDENTS ad-lib: "Way to tell him, Henry", etc.)

KENDALL. Henry, you know, don't you, that I can give you jug for that?

HENRY. I don't care.

KENDALL. I can call your mother.

HENRY. I don't care.

KENDALL. I can have you suspended.

HENRY. I don't care.

KENDALL. I can get you thrown off the basketball team.

(STUDENTS ad-lib: "Henry, man, you don't want that...")

HENRY. (*After a brief pause.*) I don't care.

KENDALL. Desirelessness. Many in the Far East strive for their entire lives to rise above their desires to the point where they "don't care." This state of utter desirelessness is called—Nirvana. But you, O my Henry, you have arrived at this exalted state in a remarkably short time in an apparently effortless way.

HENRY. I don't care.

KENDALL. Precisely.

(STUDENTS laugh, this time at Henry.)

HENRY. (*To Kendall.*) Fuck you.

(The STUDENTS react.)

KENDALL. Congratulations. You have startled your classmates. They apparently have not heard the word "fuck" before. I know the word.

HENRY. Yeah, the *word* is all you know.

KENDALL. I will admit to less knowledge of . . . well . . . "it" . . . than you, Henry. Word on the street has it that you are about to be a father.

HENRY. Not true.

KENDALL. Hard to prove.

HENRY. I can prove it.

KENDALL. How?

HENRY. I be the father of that baby, I'd be all the way to Santo Domingo by now.

KENDALL. Well, we're all entitled to our opinions.

HENRY. *It's not my kid, so fuck you!*

(The STUDENTS react.)

KENDALL. By the way, I would like to warn the class virgins that any of you "good" boys considering running to Fr. Larkin with tales of Henry's language will be hoist— repeatedly—by their own petards. What happens in this classroom is nobody's business but mine. Is that clear?

(STUDENTS mutter.)

KENDALL. IS THAT CLEAR!?!

(Reluctant agreement from STUDENTS.)

KENDALL. *(Down to serious business.)* Now, Henry, why aren't you doing my homework?

HENRY. You're a cunt.

KENDALL. *(After a brief pause.)* The word is "vagina." *(KENDALL quickly and smoothly takes a bill from his pocket and sets it on the floor in front of Henry.)* Twenty dollars if you spell it properly.

(HENRY looks at the money—wants it—looks at Kendall—looks at the money.)

KENDALL. No? *(KENDALL pockets the money.)* Henry, you are a reptile. Primate stature is wasted on you. Even so, I have a challenge for you: *Don't . . . learn . . . anything.* Do you think you can do that? For a whole year? In my class? Please, *don't learn a thing.* I have often wondered if it can be done.

HENRY. It can be done.

KENDALL. May – be, Henry, may – be. But it will be hard, Henry, because *I* am a *very* good teacher.   — bending down so to end up face to face

(School BELL freezes KENDALL and HENRY in a face off. Then, exit KENDALL.)

ACT I

Scene 6

LARKIN reenters. HENRY lingers as LARKIN discusses him.

LARKIN. Most kids you can say, "Stay in school—you'll get a better job." Not Henry. Henry works in the family business which involves selling controlled substances at inflated prices.

(Henry's BEEPER goes off. HE exits.)

LARKIN. He makes more in a day than my teachers do in a week. My faculty is living proof that a good education gets you nowhere. My teachers aren't in it for the money. My teachers are "dedicated." I *hate* dedicated teachers.

GRIFFIN. *(Entering Larkin's office.)* Thank you.

LARKIN. *(Preoccupied with office work.)* Don't thank me. Thank Mr. Kendall. He's the one who took all your classes yesterday. Sick, were you?

GRIFFIN. Yes, Father.

LARKIN. *(Preoccupied.)* Feeling better now?

GRIFFIN. Yes, Father.

LARKIN. *(Preoccupied.)* What did you have?

GRIFFIN. *(Cheerfully nasty.)* I had leukemia, you hideous Nazi.

LARKIN. *(After a brief pause.)* There's a lot of that going around these days. Usually it lasts longer, doesn't it?

GRIFFIN. I've got a strong constitution.

(School BELL rings.)

GRIFFIN. I'd better get to class. We don't want to trouble Mr. Kendall any further, now, do we?

LARKIN. Tom, could you wait one minute?

GRIFFIN. *(Exhaling.)* Sorry. Class.

LARKIN. Tom, I don't like liars.

GRIFFIN. (*Stopped dead in his tracks.*) I have a class to teach.

LARKIN. You don't have a thing to do till I say so.

GRIFFIN. Fuck you.

LARKIN. What?

GRIFFIN. Oh, excuse me. Fuck you, *Father*.

LARKIN. I'm not your father. You want to call me father, that's your problem.

GRIFFIN. I took a sick day, "Ed." I don't owe you any explanation, "Ed." Can I teach my class now, "Ed"?

LARKIN. I don't want an explanation. I want an assurance that it won't happen again.

GRIFFIN. What I do outside this school is none of your business.

LARKIN. It is if it's with a student of mine during school hours.

GRIFFIN. A student of yours, huh? How many days has he been here this past month?

LARKIN. (*After a brief pause.*) Look, you're new here. Take it a little slow.

GRIFFIN. (*On the attack.*) Nine. He's been here nine days.

LARKIN. (*Covered anger.*) You may go.

GRIFFIN. Make a difference, huh?

LARKIN. I believe you have a class.

GRIFFIN. (*Declaring war.*) What are you going to do— leave him back again at the end of the year?

LARKIN. (*The lid off Larkin's anger.*) MAYBE! *What do you want me to do?*

(*Silence.*)

GRIFFIN. (*Not a clue.*) Notify somebody.

LARKIN. OK, I will. Who do you think I should call? You know any old-time truant officers? Who? Who should I call, Tom?

GRIFFIN. (*Regaining strength.*) Fine. You go on marking him down absent every day. Fine. He's a bright kid and his education is getting flushed down the toilet.

LARKIN. And you're not going to let that happen.

GRIFFIN. No, Ed. I'm not.

(*GRIFFIN, grabbing a coat, goes to the door of Lee's apartment. It is important that there be no "real" door. STUDENTS should be used to help create a sense of the tenement, the neighborhood, the violence.*

GRIFFIN will hear voices from the other side of the door—LEE doing his mother and his brother.)

GRIFFIN. Señora? Señora?

LEE. (Tyro) WHO THE FUCK IS THAT?

GRIFFIN. My name is Griffin. I'm from Lee's school.

LEE. (Tyro) SHIT! I DON'T WANT NO FUCKING PRIEST FROM NO FUCKING TRINITY AROUND HERE. THEY COULDN'T HELP ME AND THEY'RE NOT GOING TO HELP YOU.

GRIFFIN. (*Pounding on the door.*) Señora? Señora?

LEE. (Tyro, Señora) DON'T OPEN THE DOOR. So how am I going to talk to him if I don't open the door? You want me to be like you and scream all the time? DON'T OPEN THE DOOR!

GRIFFIN. (*Shouting over.*) Look, you don't have to open the door. Just is Lee coming to school or not?

LEE. (Señora, Tyro) Yes! NO! Yes. WHERE DO YOU THINK YOU'RE GOING? I'm going to open the door so Lee can go to school 'cause if I don't open this door, I'm going to open that window and it won't be Lee that's leaving.

GRIFFIN. Señora . . .

LEE. (Tyro) WOULD YOU SHUT THE FUCK UP! I DON'T WANT ANY FAGGOT PRIESTS HANGING AROUND MY HOUSE.

GRIFFIN. *Lee has to go to school.*

LEE. (Tyro) FUCK YOU!

GRIFFIN. *Lee has to go to school so he doesn't turn out to be a shit-for-brains asshole like you!* Sorry about the language, Señora.

LEE. (Señora, Tyro) It's OK. I hear it all the time. WHAT KIND OF LANGUAGE IS THAT OUT OF A PRIEST?

GRIFFIN. I'm not a priest.

LEE. (Tyro) NO?

GRIFFIN. No.

LEE. (Tyro) THEN WHO THE FUCK ARE YOU TO TELL ME WHAT TO DO IN MY OWN APARTMENT?

GRIFFIN. OPEN THIS ...!

LEE. (*As Tyro throws the door open.*) HEY, FUCK YOU, MAN!

(LEE-as-Tyro *attacks Griffin. The fight is a brief, wildly violent apparition.* TYRO *hits Griffin in the face. The apparition disappears as* LEE *immediately turns back into* LEE.)

GRIFFIN. (*Lunging at Tyro.*) Jesus!

LEE. (*Restraining Griffin.*) Leave him alone!

GRIFFIN. (*Driving forward.*) I'm going to kill him!

LEE. (*Restraining him.*) Leave him alone! He's my *brother*.

(*School BELL, followed by a second of silence.*
We are now working in three worlds simultaneously: GRIFFIN and LARKIN are in present time; GRIFFIN and LEE continue the events of the "sick day" that Griffin took; KENDALL and JAMES continue the life of the school on the "sick day.")

KENDALL. (*Background.*) OK, gentlemen, I'll be filling in for Mr. Griffin this morning . . .

(*LARKIN reenters. STUDENTS and TEACHERS enter and stand in the shadows.*)

LARKIN. (*Inspecting Griffin's face.*) If you were in your classroom where you belonged this wouldn't have happened.

GRIFFIN. Brother? That's somebody's *brother*?

LARKIN. Tyro. He thinks with his fists. That's why I finally threw him out of here.

GRIFFIN. You threw him...? That kid needs help. How could you throw him out?

LARKIN. What was your first thought when you saw him face to face?

STUDENTS. (Tyro) YOU BETTER WATCH YOUR BACK, MAN! YOU BETTER WATCH YOUR BACK!

GRIFFIN. (*To Lee.*) Should we call the police?

LARKIN. Exactly.

LEE. For what?

STUDENTS and GRIFFIN. (Tyro) YOU BETTER *WATCH YOUR BACK!*

GRIFFIN. For that.

LEE. You can't do anything about that.

(LEE starts back to the apartment. The school day continues:)

JAMES. Let us move on to your most important subject:

KENDALL. Religion.

JAMES. No—science.

GRIFFIN. (*Exiting, to Lee*) Come on.

LEE. Where?

GRIFFIN. You're going to school.

LEE. No.

GRIFFIN. Why not?

LEE. Because.

GRIFFIN. You ever say more than two words at a time?

LEE. Yes.

LARKIN. He talked so little when he got here we assumed he didn't speak English so we put him in an all-Spanish class.

GRIFFIN. Does he speak Spanish?

LARKIN. No, but he didn't say anything about it for six months.

(The school day continues:)

KENDALL. Out of his infinite love, God created . . .

JAMES. . . . a cold mindless universe of cinders spinning in space . . .

KENDALL . . .which is governed by Divine Providence . . .

JAMES. . . . and the law of the survival of the fittest.

LEE. (*To Griffin.*) See, school makes more sense in a language you don't understand.

GRIFFIN. OK, forget school.

LARKIN. Beautiful.

GRIFFIN. Let's go some place where we can talk.

LEE. There's nothing to talk about.

GRIFFIN. Look, you need to have somebody you can talk to.

LEE. You have people like that?

GRIFFIN. Of course.

LEE. You can tell them everything?

GRIFFIN. Absolutely.

LEE. I have to go.

GRIFFIN. (*Trying to stop him.*) Lee . . .

LEE. You can tell them everything . . . you can tell them about me. (*LEE runs away.*)

LARKIN. The boy is not dumb.

(Short school BELL: STUDENTS set up comic book store during teaching.)

JAMES. All species evolved from a few common ancestors . . .

KENDALL. . . . called Adam and Eve . . .

JAMES. . . .who were probably mindless one-celled creatures . . .

KENDALL. . . .very much like you and me.

(School BELL: Comic book store.)

    LARKIN. So what did you do all day?
    LEE. *(Handing comics to Griffin.)* These.
    LARKIN. You spent the day reading *comics*?

(GRIFFIN pays for the comics.)

    LARKIN. *(Taking them from Griffin.)* Alien Hoards? Rocketbody? The New Mutants?
    GRIFFIN. *(To Larkin.)* Didn't they have these when you were young? *(GRIFFIN takes the comics from LARKIN. To Lee:)* Teenage Mutant Ninja Turtles?
    LEE. *(Taking the comics from GRIFFIN.)* Didn't they have these when you were young?
    GRIFFIN. When I *was* young? Was? *WAS*?
    LARKIN. It happens to everybody.
    GRIFFIN. *(Paging through the comics.)* No, they didn't have Teenage Ninja Mutant Turtles way back then. Besides I never much liked superheroes. I mean, how smart can they be if they have to write their names on their clothes? And look how they dress—spandex pants, little red shoes . . .

    LEE. *(Abrupt.)* Who are your heroes?
    GRIFFIN. Why?
    LEE. So I can make fun of them.
    GRIFFIN. Hard to do. I don't have any.
    LEE. No heroes?
    GRIFFIN. No.
    LEE. Then you could never understand. *(LEE runs away.)*

GRIFFIN. (*Pursuing.*) Wait a minute. Lee . . .

LARKIN. (*Heading Griffin off.*) No heroes? I'm surprised. I thought you were out to out-Jesus Jesus.

GRIFFIN. Jesus? Hell, who wants a hero who gets himself killed?

LARKIN. That's *why* he's a hero, Tom. He didn't get anybody else killed.

GRIFFIN. (*Taking a folded sheet of paper out of his pocket.*) Wait. I do have a hero. He's even a superhero.

LEE. (*Stopping.*) Who?

GRIFFIN. (*Inspecting the drawing on the paper.*) Guess.

LEE. Guess your superhero?

GRIFFIN. Yeah.

LEE. Wonder Woman.

GRIFFIN. (*Laughing.*) Fuck you.

LEE. The Silver Surfer?

GRIFFIN. No.

LEE. The X-Men?

GRIFFIN. (*Inspecting the drawing.*) No, but I can understand your not getting it 'cause he's kind of new.

LEE. (*Intrigued.*) I know all the new comics.

GRIFFIN. (*Describing the drawing.*) I bet you don't know this one. You ever see a guy in a black helmet, kind of medieval looking. Evil eyes, a sword with a chip out of it. I think his name might be "the Baron," but it's a little hard to tell because the name is just sort of scratched in . . .

LEE. (*Grabbing for the drawing.*) Where did you get that?

LARKIN. Where *did* you get that?

GRIFFIN. (*Keeping the drawing.*) Out of his desk. Have you seen this stuff? It's like urban cave painting. The kid is gifted.

LARKIN. They're all gifted. You don't know that, you shouldn't be teaching here.

LEE. *Where did you get that!*

GRIFFIN. Oh, you've seen him before. I'm surprised because I never saw him till the other day.

LEE. *Give that back.*

GRIFFIN. Oh, is it yours? You draw this, Lee?

LEE. (*After brief pause.*) No.

GRIFFIN. (*Hammering on Lee.*) Then why should I give it back to you? . . . A knight. I'm a little surprised, Lee, 'cause I thought you'd be more modern than that. A commando or a mutant or something, but no. You're an old fashioned knight. It's really well drawn, Lee, a little out of proportion but nothing that Art and Design couldn't clean up for you, but you know what? *It pisses me off.* You know why? 'Cause this is the good stuff, Lee. You've been holding out on me. See, I'm putting my ass on the line in class every day and you're holding the good shit back and that's not fair, Lee-bo. Who is this ugly fucker? This is not your standard good guy, Lee. Is it one of the teachers? Is it Fr. Larkin? *Who is the Baron?*

LEE. It's my mother, so fuck you. (*LEE, badly wounded, walks away.*)

LARKIN. His mother?

GRIFFIN. (*Instant and total remorse.*) Shit. *I'm an ASSHOLE, LEE!* I wouldn't have joked if I knew. I'm an *ASSHOLE!* Forgive me, Lee.

STUDENTS. (*Whispered.*)
SAGA AIN'T A KNIGHT WHO HAD A LOT TO SAY

'CAUSE SAGA DOESN'T WANT TO PISS HIMSELF
    AWAY.

LARKIN. The knight in the picture is his mother?

GRIFFIN. He has his whole family figured out in
mythology. The Baron is his mother and the Shadow is his
brother.

LARKIN. And who's Lee?

STUDENTS (*Whispered.*) SA - GA! SA - GA! SA -
GA!

GRIFFIN. He made me promise not to tell.

STUDENTS.

SAGA WAS BIG. SAGA WAS BUILT.

SAGA HAD TO ANSWER FOR THE BLOOD THAT
    WAS SPILT.

*(Later in the day after GRIFFIN has read the full comic of
    Saga:)*

GRIFFIN. So your mother fights with your brother?

LEE. (*Insistent on the mythology.*) No, the *Baron*—the
Baron fights with *the Shadow*.

GRIFFIN. And you break up the fights?

LEE. No *Saga. Saga* breaks up the fights.

GRIFFIN. How does he do that?

LEE. (*Delicate.*) Saga gets in the middle of the fight and
he stops it.

GRIFFIN. But how?

LEE. (*Delicate.*) By not doing anything.

GRIFFIN. Really? He doesn't fight back?

LEE. (*Delicate.*) No.

GRIFFIN. What a shitty hero!

LEE. *It takes a lot of courage not to fight back!*

GRIFFIN. (*Backing off.*) OKOKOKOKOK . . . Are there other drawings like this one?

LEE. Yes. Lots.

GRIFFIN. If they're as good as this one, Lee, you're going to have no trouble getting into Art and Design.

LEE. Miss Curry says I can't use them in my portfolio.

GRIFFIN. No?

LEE. She says they're not art.

GRIFFIN. Why not?

LEE. They're not real.

GRIFFIN. What does she think is real?

LEE. Oranges and a bottle on a table.

GRIFFIN. Lee, knights are real.

LEE. What do you know? You're an asshole.

GRIFFIN. Yes, I *am* an asshole, but I'm an asshole with a minor in history. Lee, there really were knights. They aren't like Teenage Mutant Ninja Turtles. They're real. And, Lee, this *is* art.

LEE. Yeah?

GRIFFIN. Oh, yeah.

STUDENTS. (*Strong.*) SAGA! SAGA!

(LIGHT change: Museum. STUDENTS instantaneously create the Metropolitan Museum of Art.)

GRIFFIN. Touch it.

LEE. They used swords like that?

GRIFFIN. No, they used *that*. That particular sword is 700 years old. Touch it.

LEE. The sign says don't touch.

GRIFFIN. Touch it.

LEE. I might break it.

GRIFFIN. A piece of steel that made it through the battle of Agincourt? Unlikely.

LEE. What about the guard?

GRIFFIN. The guard's a friend of mine. Step across the velvet rope and touch it.

LARKIN. Is the guard a friend of yours?

GRIFFIN. He was after I gave him twenty bucks.

LARKIN. You're teaching the kid a lie.

GRIFFIN. Well, at least I'm teaching him.

(LEE enters the world of the sword created by the STUDENTS—Saga's world.)

LEE and STUDENTS. SAGA! SAGA!

(Later in the day.)

GRIFFIN. (*Into Lee's drawings.*) Lee, I don't understand why Saga has to fight all the time.

LEE and STUDENTS.

SAGA FACES EVERY TRIAL—HE NEVER REFUSES.

SOMETIMES HE WINS BUT ONLY WHEN HE LOSES.

GRIFFIN. But how could somebody built like Saga lose all the time?

LEE AND STUDENTS.

IF YOU WIN, YOU WIN—IF YOU LOSE, YOU LOSE.

IT'S SOMETHING THAT HAPPENS—NOT SOMETHING YOU CHOOSE.

[handwritten margin note: lights on students blank faces]

GRIFFIN. Like Superman can only be hurt by Kryptonite? Like Teenage Ninja Mutant Turtles crave pizza?

LEE. Yes.

GRIFFIN. (*Breaking up Lee's fantasy world.*) *NO!* No, Lee, somebody made that stuff up.

LEE. The story's the story.

GRIFFIN. Change it.

LEE. Your family's your fate.

GRIFFIN. (*Taking over Lee's fantasy world.*) Not if you want to change it. Want anything enough, you get it. I wanted Georgetown, I got it. I didn't like it much once I got there, but wanting it got me through. Do you *want* Saga to lose to his family all the time? And who says Saga even belongs in this family? Maybe he's adopted.

(*MUSIC starts.*)

LEE. *You can't change the story!*
GRIFFIN. The hell I can't.

(*GRIFFIN, over LEE's objections, enters the rap story of Saga and, with the help of the STUDENTS, changes it.*)

GRIFFIN.
WHEN SAGA WAS A BOY HE THOUGHT THE BARON WAS HIS FATHER.
HE DIDN'T ASK QUESTIONS, I MEAN, WHY SHOULD HE BOTHER?
YOU FIND A MAN IN YOUR HOUSE—IF HE AIN'T TOO BAD

AND HE STAYS FOR A WHILE—YOU CALL THE
  DUDE DAD.
BUT SAGA'S GROWING UP. IT'S TIME FOR HIM TO
  REALIZE
THAT ALL THE BARON'S STORIES ARE LIES, LIES,
  LIES.
NOW, THE BARON'S NOT YOUR FATHER, YOU'VE
  BEEN LIVING IN DISGUISE.
IF YOU DON'T BELIEVE ME, TAKE A LOOK AT
  YOUR EYES.
    ALL .
SAGA'S EYES WERE EMPTY LIKE TWO DEEP
  HOLES.
LIKE A NIGHT WITHOUT STARS, LIKE TUNNELS
  TO HIS SOUL.
    GRIFFIN.
YOUR FATHER HAD EYES THAT DID THE SAME
  THING.
THE BARON'S NOT YOUR FATHER—YOUR
  FATHER'S *THE KING*!
    STUDENTS.
THE BARON'S NOT YOUR FATHER—YOUR
  FATHER'S *THE KING*!

(Dance break.)

    GRIFFIN.
NOW TELLING THIS TO SAGA WASN'T JUST GOOD
  NEWS.
IT WAS ALSO A WARNING—THE BOY WOULD
  HAVE TO CHOOSE.

IF THE BARON'S HIS FATHER, HE DON'T HAVE TO
    DO A THING.
BUT IT'S TIME TO CLAIM HIS CROWN IF HE'S THE
    SON OF A KING.
THE SON OF A KING.
    ALL.
THE SON OF A KING.

(Dance break.)

    ALL
SAGA, SAGA, SOMEONE PUT HIM WISE.
SAGA, SAGA, SEARCHING FOR HIS EYES.
SAGA, SAGA, TAKE A LOOK AT YOUR EYES.
SAGA WAS COOL. SAGA WAS WISE.
SAGA SAW HIS LIFE THROUGH HIS OWN PAIR OF
    EYES.
SAGA'S EYES WERE EMPTY LIKE TWO DEEP
    HOLES,
LIKE A NIGHT WITHOUT STARS,
LIKE TUNNELS TO HIS SOUL.
    LARKIN. *(Reappearing.)* He's in for a big surprise the
first time he goes to a museum without you.

(NIGHT. Silence.)

    GRIFFIN. *(Quietly.)* After the museum we went to the
Cloisters. Then to Belvedere Castle in the park. St. John
the Divine. St Patrick's. Anything even vaguely medieval
we saw.

(GRIFFIN brushes hair gently out of Lee's eyes. LEE flinches.)

LEE. Hey—what are you doing?
GRIFFIN. Relax. Take it easy.

(GRIFFIN completes what he was doing . . .and leaves his hand on Lee's face a moment longer than necessary—a presumed intimacy. Fatherly, brotherly. LEE is absolutely still.)

GRIFFIN. (*Dropping his hand.*) There. That's not so hard, is it?
LARKIN. You do anything else?
GRIFFIN. No, that's about it.

(LEE does to GRIFFIN exactly what GRIFFIN had just done to him. GRIFFIN flinches.)

GRIFFIN. (*Startled.*) Hey!
LEE. (*Imitating Griffin.*) Relax.

(LEE completes his motion, and leaves his hand on Griffin's face a moment longer than necessary.)

LEE. (*Knowing how hard such intimacy is.*) There. That's not so hard. Is it? (*LEE runs off.*)

(GRIFFIN collapses.
LARKIN approaches Griffin and puts his hand on Griffin's shoulder paternally, giving GRIFFIN another start.)

LARKIN. (*Honestly.*) Tom, I . . . I want you to teach here next year.

GRIFFIN. What?

LARKIN. I know you've got other possibilities that'll pay better and all. Graduate school, maybe. But I want you to stay here.

GRIFFIN. (*Astonished.*) Are you kidding?

LARKIN. (*Self-disclosing with difficulty.*) I'm not somebody who shows my feelings easily. A lot of people are misled by that. It's important to me that you understand that I like you . . . I admire you . . . and, in time, I think I could come to think of you as . . . a son. Have I offended you?

GRIFFIN. No, I just don't know what to say.

LARKIN. (*Warm.*) Surprised?

GRIFFIN. Yes . . . Moved.

LARKIN. Really.

GRIFFIN. Yes, I'm sorry . . . I don't know what to say.

LARKIN. (*Coming out of his act.*) But you are just about ready to eat out of my hand?

GRIFFIN. What?

LARKIN. (*Firmly.*) Tom. *Affection is coercion.*

GRIFFIN. (*Blowing up.*) YOU HAVE GOT NO RIGHT TO PLAY WITH ME LIKE THAT!

LARKIN. *It's exactly what you are doing with that kid.*

GRIFFIN. *I'm not playing with him! I like him!*

LARKIN. *DON'T! DON'T LIKE HIM! IT LEAVES HIM NO FREEDOM!* His mother got the shit beaten out of her yesterday.

GRIFFIN. Yeah?

LARKIN. *Yeah.* If Lee had been home it wouldn't have happened.

GRIFFIN. If Lee had been home it would have happened to *him*.

LARKIN. No sympathy for her?

GRIFFIN. I've got a limited supply.

LARKIN. Tom . . . there's a kind of ecology of evil in the neighborhood and it doesn't take much to upset it. Offer a cup of coffee to a whore in front of the building. One day, OK. Do it two days in a row—give her something to look forward to—see how fast the balance is upset.

GRIFFIN. (*Biting.*) Wouldn't want to upset the pimps now, would we, Ed?

LARKIN. (*Matching him.*) Look, fights here aren't like on a college basketball court or like on TV where they last for twenty minutes. Fights here are twenty seconds—thirty tops—then it's over. Real over.

GRIFFIN. I can take care of myself.

LARKIN. *That's what you think this is about? You? Yourself?* You upset the balances in that family and that kid could get *killed*.

GRIFFIN. *How would you know what upsets the balances? When did you ever knock on his door?*

LARKIN. *Can you handle what's on the other side of that door?*

GRIFFIN. *It's not that hard. It's getting a kid to school.*

LARKIN. You know, you ought to keep your eyes open and your mouth shut.

GRIFFIN. Kind of opposite of you, huh, Ed?

LARKIN. Go to your class. Go teach what little you know.

GRIFFIN. (*A vow.*) *All I know is that he'll be in school. Every day. For the rest of the term.*

(Short school BELL: exit GRIFFIN.)

LARKIN. And he was in school. On time. Homework done. For a couple of weeks. Asked some pretty good questions, too. Like—if in English and math two negatives always make a positive, how come in religion, two wrongs never make a right? I didn't have a clue. Told him I'd get back to him the next day. But he was absent the next day...

GRIFFIN. *(Running to Lee's door.)* Come on, Lee . . .

LARKIN. . . . and the next . . .

GRIFFIN. . . . You've only missed a couple of days now . . .

LARKIN. . . . and the next. *(Exit LARKIN.)*

GRIFFIN. Let's get back on track. Come on. Let's go to St. Mark's Comix.

LEE. *(Appearing, beaten.)* You called somebody.

GRIFFIN. I didn't. I swear to God. Jesus Christ, Lee, what happened to you?

LEE. *(A violent trance.)* Somebody called somebody or wrote to somebody and they sent somebody here to talk to my mother and they said she had to prove that she was a fit mother. WHO ARE THEY TO SAY IF I'M A FIT MOTHER? And so she gets upset and when she gets upset she drinks. HOW MANY CHILDREN YOU GOT? I GOT FOUR. FOUR CHILDREN. Then she gets mad and sets fire to things. THEY'RE MY THINGS. I CAN DO WHAT I WANT WITH THEM. So I have to stay home and make sure that nothing happens to the kids. GET OUT. So I pretend to be sick. *GET OUT*. But she can tell when I pretend. *GET OUT!* So I have to *get* sick. I can get sick pretty easy now. I can get a fever just by wanting one.

Want to see? So you and Fr. Larkin think you're making
things better, but you're not. You're just making me sick.

GRIFFIN. Look, you're coming with me.

LEE. (*Absolute clarity.*) DON'T YOU LISTEN TO
ANYTHING I SAY AT ALL? DON'T HELP! GO AWAY!
GET AWAY FROM MY APARTMENT AND DON'T
COME BACK. THIS IS MORE IMPORTANT THAN
SCHOOL OR SOME MUSEUM. LEAVE—US—
ALONE! JUST LEAVE US ALONE!

(LEE exits. STUDENTS run frantically across stage to get
to class, preventing GRIFFIN from reaching Lee.
LARKIN enters quietly.)

GRIFFIN. Did you call?

LARKIN. (*After brief pause.*) Yes.

GRIFFIN. *WHY?*

LARKIN. You told me to, Tom . . . Didn't you? . . .
You convinced me it might be worth the try.

GRIFFIN. (*After a pause.*) So it is my fault. (*Pause.*
GRIFFIN sits.) Ah, shit.

LARKIN. Funny thing happens down here, Tom.
Bunch of upwardly-mobiles buy a tenement, clean it up, let
some light in, truck hits a pothole, the building falls
down. Happens regularly. Sometimes it's the dirt that holds
the whole thing together.

GRIFFIN. (*After a pause.*) Bless me, father, for I have
fucked up.

LARKIN. (*Consoling.*) It happens . . . I fucked up with
Tyro . . . With a lot of Tyros.

GRIFFIN. Is that supposed to make me feel better?

LARKIN. (*Hurt, smiling.*) I guess not.

GRIFFIN. I'm sorry.

LARKIN. I believe you have a class.

GRIFFIN. What good does class do a kid like Lee?

LARKIN. (*Honest and simple.*) I don't know—what good your field trip do him? Look, Tom, you're not a half-bad teacher, but if you're going to teach *down here* it's important to respect what happens when you fuck with the ecology. (*Building energy for the meeting that follows:*) Teach, teach, and *teach some more.*

(*School BELL.*)

ACT I

Scene 7

School BELL: a teachers' meeting.

LARKIN and TEACHERS. Father. Son. Holy Spirit . . . Prayer.

TEACHERS. Amen.

LARKIN. (*All brisk business.*) Reports from committees—

JAMES. Request for salary increase for the lay faculty.

LARKIN. Good work you're doing, guys. Hell of a job. Not a chance. Next topic.

JAMES. Request for introduction of sex education courses into second term curriculum.

LARKIN. Denied. This is a Catholic school—the kids don't officially know anything about sex till they're eighteen. And then it's forbidden.

KENDALL. Request for reconsideration.

LARKIN. Do we need it?

KENDALL. Jose Ortiz is taking birth control pills—you tell me.

LARKIN. (*Bulldozing*.) I'll think about it. Marking period closes the Wednesday before Thanksgiving. Marks will be due that morning. Any discussion? Teacher attendance at morning mass has been excellent with one notable exception. Any discussion? Any kids to be discussed?

(HANDS shoot into the air.)

LARKIN. Mitch?

JAMES. I'd like to discuss Henry Rodriguez.

(HENRY enters. Other STUDENTS appear about the set.)

LARKIN. OK.

JAMES. I want him suspended—by the thumbs if possible.

LARKIN. What did he do?

JAMES. He put a tampon in my grade book.

(STUDENTS cheer.)

LARKIN. Suspended.

(HENRY—angry—and STUDENTS exit.)

KENDALL. Objection.

LARKIN. Burke?

KENDALL. If a teacher can't control a class maybe it isn't the class's problem.

LARKIN. That's enough, Burke.

JAMES. No, let him have his say.

KENDALL. SIT DOWN! BE QUIET! SHUT UP! STOP THAT! What could they possibly be doing to make you scream that way? Even if they were to say as I once heard through the wall—that your mother was giving away her funky pussy on Delancey Street because nobody'd buy it on Second Avenue, what does it take away from you (or—for that matter—from your mother's allegedly funky pussy) to just let them *say* it and move on?

JAMES. I guess I'm not like you, I suppose. I try to get a certain amount of *work* done every day. I can't stop and "talk it out" each time a problem comes up. I hear your classes through the wall too.

LARKIN. That's enough.

JAMES. Besides, just talk to the boy. He has no interest in being here. He told me that himself.

KENDALL. (*Strong advocacy.*) He tells everybody that and he still turns up every day. Perfect attendance, Ed.

JAMES. *So what*? He's not learning anything. He's a complete illiterate.

KENDALL. (*Turning on James.*) Yes. Yes he is, but when he arrived here he was practically *averbal,* so, for Henry, *illiteracy* is an *achievement.* All things considered, I think it's quite an accomplishment—*especially with you screaming at him all the time.*

JAMES. You know, I wish you'd treat me like a child. You get along with them so much better than you do with your peers.

KENDALL. Why don't we just compare standardized test scores at the end of the year?

JAMES. *Gladly!*

LARKIN. Tom, do you have anything to add?

GRIFFIN. Henry? Throw him out of the lifeboat. Mitch wants him out in the name of education so he's going to go sooner or later. Why fight the inevitable?

JAMES. I'm not inventing this issue. Henry is a problem.

GRIFFIN. Mitch, let me ask you a question—who's this school for if not for Henry?

JAMES. The kids who want to learn.

GRIFFIN. They'll get educated perfectly well without us. You want to know what the real purpose of this school is?

JAMES. What?

GRIFFIN. To keep the teachers off the street.

LARKIN. We make a difference.

GRIFFIN. Do we, Ed? Do we?

JAMES. Furthermore, I suspect Henry of stealing.

LARKIN. Stealing?

JAMES. Word has it that it was Henry who took Lionel's coat.

KENDALL. *Lionel stole it in the first place, so let's not make a federal case out of it!*

GRIFFIN. *Forget the coat. You don't care about the goddamn coat.* It's just a *COAT*, Goddamn it! I'll *pay* for the coat. Let's talk about the empty desks we're teaching.

LARKIN. Our dropout rate is considerably better than the national . . .

GRIFFIN. AND I DON'T CARE ABOUT THE NUMBERS! I'M SICK OF SAYING SOMETHING'S *WRONG* AND HAVING THE *NUMBERS* QUOTED TO ME. "I FEEL SICK THIS MORNING." "OH REALLY, WELL THIRTY-SEVEN PERCENT OF ALL TEACHERS HAVE A HEAD COLD ON ANY GIVEN DAY OF SCHOOL." SO WHAT? SO FUCKING WHAT IF WE'RE ABOVE OR BELOW THE AVERAGE? I'M TALKING ABOUT KIDS—ONE AT A TIME.

KENDALL. Tantrum time.

GRIFFIN. Shut up, Burke.

JAMES. What's wrong with him?

KENDALL. He can't get Lee Cortez to school, I don't know—what would you say, Tom?—fifty percent of the time?

JAMES. Look, Tom, there's nothing wrong with caring about a kid, but don't waste your time on one from a bad family. Pick reasonable odds.

LARKIN. Much as I hate to say it, Mitch is right.

JAMES. Thank you.

LARKIN. Lee's home situation is impossible.

GRIFFIN. OK, so we work with the family.

LARKIN. (*Subtly suckering Griffin.*) Oh yeah! Oh, good! Great idea! GREAT idea! Work with the . . . Why haven't I thought of that before? How will we start?

GRIFFIN. (*Pleased with Larkin's response.*) I don't know. Adult education?

LARKIN. Adult ed? . . . What a great idea! Get the parents involved in the educational process?

GRIFFIN. (*Enthused.*) Yeah.

LARKIN. Great. Great. But wait! I forgot—I forgot—most of the parents can't come at night. They've got to work second jobs since their day jobs as janitors and waiters don't pay and that's especially bad when the people who own those businesses and restaurants start buying their buildings and forcing the rent from two-fifty to a thousand two-fifty.

GRIFFIN. Look . . .

LARKIN. So I tell you what! Let's get some housing lawyers down here and, say, while we're at it, let's organize a city-wide rent strike by the Latino community. *Yeah*! And—hey!—if we can pull that off, that just might give us the political clout we need to get *the police* to stop pussyfooting around with the hookers and the dealers in the neighborhood . . .

GRIFFIN. Ed . . .

LARKIN. . . . but, what the hell, that's just scratching the surface 'cause the local police can't do much about drugs since it's the *federal* government that's looking the other way to let the drugs pour in, so we'd better go down to *Washington! Yeah!* BUT WAIT!—*I forgot*! The federal government already *HAS* a big-money war on drugs which—hell!—even if it's only HALF as effective as HUD's war on homelessness—ought to set education back ten years—*BUT WAIT*!—I *FORGOT*!—WE ALREADY SPENT *DOUBLE* THE DRUG BUDGET TO INVADE PANAMA TO BUST ONE—REALLY—*ONE*! PUSHER AND WHATEVER OTHER MONEY THEY CAN FIND IS GOING TO HAVE TO GO TO THE SAVINGS AND LOANS *ANYWAY*—SO YOU KNOW WHAT WE REALLY OUGHT TO DO—YOU AND ME, TOM? YOU KNOW WHAT WE *REALLY* OUGHT TO DO? WE

OUGHT TO RAISE ENOUGH MONEY TO AIRLIFT ALL OUR KIDS TO *JAPAN* FOR A FEW YEARS AND THEN *MAYBE*, JUST *MAYBE*, THEY *MIGHT* HAVE A CHANCE *TO LEARN HOW TO READ BEFORE THEY START HAVING BABIES THEMSELVES*! (*LARKIN exiting slams a locker* hard.) JESUS!

(KENDALL, pleased, exits, leaving JAMES at his locker and GRIFFIN sitting with his head in his hands. Silence. Then GRIFFIN looks up with a smile:)

GRIFFIN. OK, Ed, let's *do* that. Let's fuck up that old ecology of evil. What else is life for?

JAMES. (*Pouring a drink for himself.*) Tommy, Tommy, Tommy. Don't take it too hard.

GRIFFIN. Just another day of teaching, huh, Mitch?

JAMES. You know the best definition of teaching I ever heard? Casting fake pearls before real swine. Have a drink? (*JAMES pours for Griffin.*) You know, you're trying to change something that isn't supposed to change. Everybody *knows* what's going on. It's no *accident* that the drop-out rate is seventy percent.

GRIFFIN. Spare me the cynicism, Mitch.

JAMES. Hey, I'm not a cynic—I'm a historian.

GRIFFIN. You teach physics.

JAMES. I would never teach anything I cared as much about as history and—as an *American* historian—I tell you that nothing is going to change. People go to the movies, they rent videos and they take naps. Did you know that America's major contribution to western civilization is the nap? Yeah, we're the sleepiest people in the history of the world. Have another. Nothing changes. And you know why? Because things *are* the way they're *supposed* to be.

GRIFFIN. (*Loosening up over a drink.*) And why is that, Mitch?

JAMES. Somebody has to pick up the garbage. Hell, at least with the Indians we needed the land.

GRIFFIN. (*Laughing.*) You make me sick.

JAMES. (*Pouring.*) You think you have higher ideals than I do.

GRIFFIN. True.

JAMES. And that's where you're different from me.

GRIFFIN. (*Toasting.*) Vive la difference.

(*THEY drink.*)

JAMES. Yeah, well, you may be right. You know where I'm different from you?

GRIFFIN. Where?

JAMES. At the end of the year, when you're gone? I'll still be here teaching them. Bye! (*Exit JAMES.*)

(*Enter STUDENTS around a somewhat drunk GRIFFIN.*)

STUDENTS.
YOU CROSS A LION AND AN EAGLE AND IN THE
    BOOKS I'VE READ
IT SAYS YOU GET A LION'S BODY WITH AN
    EAGLE'S HEAD.
BUT AFTER ALL THAT TROUBLE, YOU GOT TO
    WONDER WHY
'CAUSE IT LOOKS GREAT ON PAPER BUT *IT'S
    NEVER GONNA FLY*.

(GRIFFIN, quite drunk, arrives at his apartment.)

ACT I

Scene 8

GRIFFIN calls his father.

GRIFFIN. Yes, I'd like to speak with Mr. John Griffin, please. This is his son, Tom. TOMMY, GOOD TO HEAR FROM YOU. Sorry to call so late. I called your house—Diane told me you were still at the office. I hope I'm not interrupting. NO, ALWAYS GLAD TO HEAR FROM YOU TOM. I need a favor, Dad. NO MONEY, TOM. I TOLD YOU WHEN YOU TOOK THAT JOB, TOM. THE MONEY I SPENT ON YOUR EDUCATION, TOM. REAL WORLD JOB, TOM. HISPANICS REFUSE TO LEARN ENGLISH. WELFARE STATE. SECURE BORDERS, TOM. THIRD WORLD DEBT, TOM. Look, I'm not calling for money, Dad. Dad, would you mind calling . . . *(Shooting his brains out with a finger.)* . . . the law school admissions office for me? I'M VERY HAPPY TO HEAR THAT, TOM. VERY HAPPY. VERY HAPPY INDEED. Yeah, I thought you would be. SO, YOU WANT TO BE A LAWYER. NO! No, dad, NO! Nobody *wants* to be a lawyer, Dad. That's why they have to pay them so much . . . But maybe I better start thinking about it, dad. *(Starting to cry with loss.)* See, I always thought I'd have a life, Dad, but now maybe I'll just have a career instead . . . No, I'm fine, Dad, fine. It's just that I'm not doing anybody any good around here and if I'm going to waste my life, I might as well at least be able to bill the time to somebody. (*Hangs up. Throws up.*) I'd *like* to be able to *help* somebody—but *nobody's willing to fight*—Goddamn it!

(*LEE—with two boxes of comics—is knocking hard on Griffin's apartment door.*)

LEE. Mr. Griffin?

GRIFFIN. Go away!

LEE. I need your help.

GRIFFIN. So what? I needed your help and where were you? I promised Larkin that you'd be in school *every day.* You've been out for *three weeks! You made a fool out of me, kid.*

LEE. (*Knocking harder on the door.*) I need a place to leave my comics.

GRIFFIN. So what? I told you to get out . . .

LEE. *I need a place to leave my comics.*

GRIFFIN. (*Going to door.*) Shit. (*GRIFFIN throws the door open.*) YOU'RE . . . (*Stopped by the sight of Lee.*) . . . you're bleeding.

LEE. (*Bringing the comics in.*) No, I'm not.

GRIFFIN. Look at your shirt.

LEE. It's not my blood.

GRIFFIN. Whose is it?

LEE. Tyro's. It's Tyro's blood. I did what you told me. I changed the story.

GRIFFIN What did you do?

LEE. (*Quiet, but deeply excited.*) I killed my brother.

GRIFFIN. (*After brief pause.*) Oh, my God!

LEE. Just like you told me to.

GRIFFIN. Oh, shit. You killed him?

LEE. Isn't that what you told me to do?

GRIFFIN. Oh, man. Oh, my God! You killed him?

LEE. Yeah. I shot him.

GRIFFIN. You . . .

LEE. No, I stabbed him.

GRIFFIN. What?

LEE. No, I threw him off the Empire State Building.

GRIFFIN. What did you do?

LEE. Mr. Griffin, I changed the story. *I beat up my brother.*

GRIFFIN. That's all?

LEE. That's *all*? I beat him till he bled.

GRIFFIN. Oh, Christ. Christ, don't ever do that to me again . . .

LEE. You can't tell me what to do. Nobody can. I can do what I want. I can change the story.

GRIFFIN. Why did you beat him up?

LEE. You told me to.

GRIFFIN. I didn't . . .

LEE. You know those voices in my head—you're one of them now. That sound funny?

GRIFFIN. Not really. I've heard you more than once too.

LEE. I've got to go. Take care of my comics. (*LEE moves for the door.*)

GRIFFIN. (*Getting into it.*) Wait a minute. Stay and celebrate. You kicked that fucker's ass? That's GREAT, Lee! That's *FANTASTIC!*

LEE. It's not great—I'm not supposed to beat up my brother.

GRIFFIN. What are you supposed to do?

LEE. Get between him and my mother and let them fight till he's tired then we all go to sleep on the bed. But this time I got mad and I hit him.

GRIFFIN. Great!

LEE. IT'S NOT GREAT!

GRIFFIN. Yes, it is. It's *terrific*.

LEE. (*Hits Griffin hard.*) There! Is that great! Is it? Is that great! (*LEE hits Griffin again.*)

GRIFFIN. LEE!

(LEE stops.)

GRIFFIN. What did your brother do when you hit him?

LEE. (*Himself, then Señora.*) The same as you. He just stood there. So I thought, "Shit, I might not get a chance like this again." So I hit him. I hit him again. And again. And again. You know where his face goes in here? I could feel my fist go right in there like it was made to fit! LEAVE HIM ALONE! OYE! LEAVE HIM ALONE!

GRIFFIN. Why did you stop?

LEE. My mother threw me out.

GRIFFIN. She threw YOU out? Why did she throw YOU out?

LEE. (*Señora, then himself.*) YOUR BROTHER IS BLEEDING! SO WHAT HE'S BLEEDING? YOU DON'T THROW HIM OUT WHEN I'M BLEEDING! GET OUT! GET OUT! I have to go back. (*LEE runs for the door.*)

GRIFFIN. (*On fire to do something.*) Look, I'll call the police . . .

LEE. You can't . . .

GRIFFIN. I'll call Father Larkin . . .

LEE. You can't tell anybody about this . . .

GRIFFIN. Look, if you're going to go, I'll go back with you. . .

LEE. I DON'T WANT YOU TO COME WITH ME!

GRIFFIN. So what am I supposed to do? Stay here and do nothing?

LEE. ALL I WANT YOU TO DO IS KEEP MY COMICS!

GRIFFIN. (*Kicking the comics.*) WHO THE FUCK CARES ABOUT YOUR COMICS? Jesus Christ, Lee, they're like fucking roach farms. I'm just going to put them in the hall . . .

LEE. (*Hitting him.*) *You said they could stay . . .*

GRIFFIN. What do you think you're . . .

LEE. (*Hitting him again.*) *You said they could stay here!*

(*GRIFFIN, hit too hard, explodes.*)

GRIFFIN. *Shit, kid, you're going to get it.*

(*LEE hits him again.*
When GRIFFIN goes to hit LEE, LEE falls to the floor.
GRIFFIN catches himself before the punch is thrown.
LEE, seeing GRIFFIN's hesitation, screams:)

LEE. *HIT ME! HIT ME! HIT ME! HIT ME! HITTTTTTTT MEEEEEEEEEE!*

(GRIFFIN grabs the boy and holds him tight until LEE,
*   spent, collapses into GRIFFIN's arms.*
Meanwhile, MARCO and LARKIN have begun morning
*   mass—MARCO singing a hymn.*
GRIFFIN puts LEE to bed in GRIFFIN's apartment.)

ACT I

Scene 9

LARKIN. *(With purple stole.)* Early mass this morning
is being offered in loving memory of Octavio de la
Cuadra—some of you knew him. He was one of our recent
graduates who never caught on to the meaning of
responsibility. God have mercy on his soul 'cause some
son of a bitch didn't have much mercy on his body. The
Lord be with you.

(ALARM CLOCK rings: GRIFFIN's apartment, weeks
*   later. LEE still drowsy in bed; GRIFFIN rushing to get*
*   ready for school.)*

GRIFFIN. *(Picking up Lee's clothes.)* Why are you still
in bed? Come on. You're going to be late for school. And
start picking up after yourself. I'm getting sick of you
treating this place like it was the Grand Hyatt and the
maid'll be through in a minute.

(As LEE dresses, he will put on better clothes than he has
*   had till this point. GRIFFIN continues to pick up.)*

LEE. (*Sleepy and cranky.*) I'm not going to school today.

GRIFFIN. (*Getting LEE up.*) Oh, yes, you are. How late did you stay up last night?

LEE. Late.

GRIFFIN. Did you get your homework done?

LEE. I had things on my mind.

GRIFFIN. Did you pick a book for Mr. Kendall's report?

LEE. Which one should I do?

GRIFFIN. Pick a short one. Did you at least get Mr. James' assignment done?

LEE. I told you—I had things on my . . .

GRIFFIN. OK, that's it. That's it. This is my house—*my house*—and here you have to play by *my* rules, understand? No TV tonight—no stereo—no *nothing* till your homework's done.

LEE. You can't make rules for me.

LARKIN. (*Mass, which will continue off and on throughout the scene.*) In the name of the Father . . .

LEE. You're not my father.

LARKIN. . . . and of the Son . . .

GRIFFIN. And you're not my son . . .

LARKIN. . . .and the Holy Spirit.

GRIFFIN. If you were my son, you'd be white and smart.

LARKIN. Amen.

LEE. Yeah? Only if you had a real smart wife.

GRIFFIN. (*Laughing.*) Fuck you.

LEE. (*Laughing.*) Fuck you.

LARKIN. And the Lord be with *you.*

HENRY. (*Running in wildly.*) *And fuck you too!*

(*A sudden fight between HENRY and JAMES. GRIFFIN separates a furious JAMES and a defiant HENRY. STUDENTS follow cheering.*)

JAMES. Fuck you.

HENRY. Fuck you.

JAMES. Fuck you.

LARKIN. *Never let the student set the tone of the discussion.*

JAMES. I'm sorry but this is *intolerable.*

LARKIN. What is the cause of this "debate"?

KENDALL. (*Enjoying this.*) Well, from what I heard . . . In science class Mr. James said that everyone in the room was a homo sapiens.

HENRY. (*Explosive.*) Fuck him.

KENDALL. Henry took exception to that . . . He said that while he knew *some* people in the room were definitely homo sapiens, he was not one of them. Then he then tried to make Mr. James *eat* volume H of the Encyclopedia Britannica. Nothing serious.

JAMES. Nothing serious!?! CHRIST!

ALL. CHRIST!

LARKIN. (*Returning to the mass.*) Christ, have mercy.

ALL. Christ, have mercy.

LARKIN. Lord, have mercy.

ALL. Lord, have mercy.

LARKIN. Christ, have mercy.

ALL. Christ, have mercy.

(*School BELL: STUDENTS form a class.*)

KENDALL. Lee, your report, please.

LEE. It isn't ready.

KENDALL. No extensions, Lee, you know that.

GRIFFIN. Oh, come on. Give him a break.

LARKIN. (*Mass.*) Lord, have mercy.

ALL. Lord, have mercy.

LARKIN. Christ, have mercy.

ALL. Christ, have mercy.

GRIFFIN. Mr. Kendall, have mercy.

ALL. Mr. Kendall, have mercy.

KENDALL. Oh, very well.

(That night: GRIFFIN and LEE at Griffin's apartment.)

GRIFFIN. He gave you an extension. Write it!

LEE. I can't.

GRIFFIN. Finish the report and I'll give you ten dollars.

LEE. I don't want ten dollars.

GRIFFIN. OK, what do you want?

LEE. (*After brief pause.*) I want to spend Thanksgiving with your family.

GRIFFIN. (*Touched.*) Yeah?

LEE. Yeah.

GRIFFIN. Deal. Write the report tonight.

LEE. I can't tonight. I haven't read the book.

GRIFFIN. What's that got to do with it? I got some of my best marks on books I never read.

(School BELL: class, next morning.)

KENDALL. Your report please, Lee.

GRIFFIN. Look I'll tell you the story . . .

KENDALL. Lee?

GRIFFIN. (*Leading LEE who repeats line by line, overlapping.*) The Odyssey is about a bunch of warriors who take a trip.

LEE. The Odyssey is about a bunch of warriors who take a trip . . .

GRIFFIN. (*As LEE continues to repeat line by line overlapping.*) They go through many adventures together. They go to an island where a woman turns men into animals, an island of drugs, an island of one-eyed men.

LEE. . . . an island of one eyed men . . .This isn't going to work.

GRIFFIN. Go on, there's a trick . . .

KENDALL. Lee?

LEE. Not with Mr. Kendall. With Mr. Kendall, even if you *read* the book he keeps asking questions till you get one wrong.

KENDALL. Go on.

GRIFFIN. Most of the story is about battles and suffering . . .

LEE. Most of the story is about battles and suffering.

KENDALL. Yes?

LEE. What's the trick?

GRIFFIN. Make it personal. Break his heart. That's all any liberal arts teacher ever wants.

LEE. Mr. Kendall doesn't have a heart.

GRIFFIN. Trust me.

KENDALL. (*Annoyed.*) LEE!

LEE. When the hero finally gets home, he finds his family is a bigger battle than all the other battles combined . . . Is that personal enough?

GRIFFIN. Not even close.

KENDALL. Good. Now some questions . . . .

GRIFFIN. Do it.

LEE. I'm not done.

GRIFFIN. Do it!

LEE. (*After brief pause—utter sincerity.*) I like this book—because it is just like my life.

GRIFFIN. (*After brief pause.*) Watch!

KENDALL. (*After brief pause, moved.*) My, my . . .

GRIFFIN. (*Delighted.*) See!

KENDALL. Lee, that was an excellent report!

HENRY. (*Disgusted.*) "I like this book because it is just like my life?"

(*HENRY barfs.*)

KENDALL. Henry, you take jug this afternoon. Nice work, Lee. (*Exit KENDALL.*)

GRIFFIN. Nice work, Lee. (*Exit GRIFFIN.*)

HENRY. Nice work, Lee. "I like this book because it is just like my life." Bull—fucking—shit.

(*HENRY jumps LEE. STUDENTS get involved in the melee.*)

LARKIN. (*Shouting over the fight—Mass again.*) *Let us exchange with one another the sign of Christ's Peace.*

(Sudden soupy holiday MUSIC.
Thanksgiving at Griffin's house. Full cast creates the
household.)

MOTHER/KENDALL. Oh, so this is the Lee we've all
been hearing so much about!!!

GRIFFIN. Lee, I'd like you to meet my family. My
mother . . .

MOTHER/KENDALL. Now don't just stand there,
Tom, bring Lee inside!

GRIFFIN. My father . . .

FATHER/JAMES. Nice to meet you—will dinner be
over before the game?

GRIFFIN. My brothers . . . .

BROTHER 1/CARLOS. He's staying in my room.

BROTHER 2/MARCO. No, he's not—he's staying
with me.

BROTHER 1/CARLOS. Your room is a mess.

BROTHER 2/MARCO. Yeah, well, so's yours.

MOTHER/KENDALL. Now don't start fighting first
thing!

FATHER/JAMES. OK, boys, listen to your mother.

GRIFFIN. And this is my grandmother.

GRANDMOTHER/LARKIN. Hello, dear.

FATHER/JAMES. Is dinner ready?

MOTHER/KENDALL. Yes.

ALL. Blessusohlordandthesethygiftsamen.

(ALL sit. Then, at increasing speed:)

ALL. Turkeypotatoessaladstuffingturkeyopotoesaladstu
ffingturkeypotatoessaladstuffingturkeypotatoessaladstuffing.

(Enormous sigh of satisfaction.)

FATHER/JAMES. *(As KENDALL clears the table.)*
God, that was good. I ate too much . . .

GRANDMOTHER/LARKIN. You always eat too
much.

FATHER/JAMES. Would you talk to your mother,
please?

GRANDMOTHER/LARKIN. Well, he does always eat
too much . . .

BROTHER 2/MARCO. Lee, you play basketball?

BROTHER 1/CARLOS. No, let's play video games.

MOTHER/KENDALL. No! Let's see those *drawings*
we've all heard so much about.

(LEE slowly reveals one of his drawings.)

FAMILY. Oooooooooooohhhhhhhhhhhhhhh!

BROTHER 1/CARLOS. Oh, man. They're great. . . .

BROTHER 2/MARCO. Awesome, Lee.

BROTHER 3/FREDDY. That's neato.

GRANDMOTHER/LARKIN. That picture's *ugly*.

(The FAMILY tries to quiet GRANDMOTHER.)

GRIFFIN. Don't say that, gram.

GRANDMOTHER/LARKIN. I've lived here *all my life*
and I'll say what I *damn well please*. It's all fighting and
killing.

GRIFFIN. There's kissing too, gram—you like that.

GRANDMOTHER/LARKIN. Not when they have their *mouths open!* Honestly, I don't know WHERE young people these days get such IDEAS!

BROTHER 2/MARCO. Come on, gram, didn't you ever french gramps?

GRANDMOTHER/LARKIN. (*Outraged.*) Did I ever french...? Are you going to let him talk to me like that?

BROTHER 1/CARLOS. Let me take a picture.

(As the FAMILY arranges itself for a photo, everyone gets involved in a fight between the parents.)

MOTHER/KENDALL. That's enough drinks, John.

FATHER/JAMES. I just had two.

MOTHER/KENDALL. (*With an edge.*) Three, John, I've been counting.

FATHER/JAMES. (*More of an edge.*) Oh, you've been counting, have you?

MOTHER/KENDALL. (*Escalating.*) We'll talk about this *later*.

FATHER/JAMES. We'll talk about it right . . .

BROTHER 1/CARLOS. OK. Picture, everybody. Smile!

(A sudden group smile!
Snap!
The happy FAMILY freezes into the photo.
LEE slowly steps out of the picture to look at it and, as he does, the picture dissolves.
Griffin's apartment, night:)

GRIFFIN. I said go to bed.

LEE. (*Deep within himself.*) You can't make rules for me.

GRIFFIN. I know, I know, I'm not your father.

LEE. That's right. If you were my father you wouldn't be a cold white boy like you are. You'd be dark and macho like me.

GRIFFIN. (*Amused.*) It's taken you all this time to come up with that, hasn't it?

LEE. Leave me alone.

GRIFFIN. You know you haven't said ten civil words to me since we got back from Thanksgiving.

LEE. So what?

GRIFFIN. I guess I shouldn't have asked you home. I thought you'd have a good time.

LEE. I had a good time. I didn't know families could be like that.

GRIFFIN. I know, things got a little rough. My mother never should have invited my father . . .

LEE. That's not it. I liked your family. It's that . . .

GRIFFIN. What?

LEE. You know how it makes my family look?

GRIFFIN. (*Moving towards Lee.*) Ah, Lee . . .

(*LARKIN appears—urgent agenda. Controlled, but outraged to the point of almost finding his predicament funny.*
Griffin's apartment/Larkin's office overlapping.)

LARKIN. Tom . . . could I speak to you?

GRIFFIN. (*Still focused on Lee.*) In a minute.

LARKIN. Not a minute. *Now*, Tom. Lee's mother is downstairs asking where her son is living.

(LEE runs to check out his mother.)

LARKIN. When I told her I didn't know, she said I should ask *you.*

LEE. (*Panic.*) Fr. Larkin always tries to make things better, but he only makes them worse.

LARKIN. (*To Griffin.*) Well?

LEE. Two years ago he found out that I wasn't baptized, so he baptized me . . .

LARKIN. Tom?

LEE. Before he baptized me, I never sinned at all. Now I sin all the time. How does that make it better?

LARKIN. He's got to go back, Tom.

GRIFFIN. Go back?

LARKIN. Yes.

GRIFFIN. (*Astonished.*) You're pissed at me.

LARKIN. Pissed? No, I'm not pissed. I'm fucking *enraged.*

GRIFFIN. Man, you ought to be giving me a medal.

LARKIN. Not only is it unprofessional, it's *unethical* and I hate to think of the legal complications. How could you possibly do such a thing?

LEE. I *liked* your house, Mr. Griffin. I liked playing with your brothers. We play different games at our house. They only start like games.

(GRIFFIN and LEE pass a basketball playfully to punctuate the story. As the story progresses, the passes become increasingly violent.)

LEE. Like one time, my little brother thought he was just fooling around and he screamed that I hit him. He screamed and my mother started to chase me around the apartment. That was *like* a game. But then she started to get mad because she couldn't catch me. See, I hid behind a table. I thought I'd be safe with the table between me and her, but she started to push the table against the wall. (*Dead stop.*) I never told this to anybody before. (*Passes become more violent.*) She pushed the table against the wall again and again. And I couldn't hide, see. I tried to go down under the table and when I tried, the table hit my head and she kept hitting the table against the wall . . . (*Pounding the ball into the floor*) . . . again and again and again and again . . . (*Silence.*) I can't go back there. I won't go back there, Mr. Griffin. (*LEE exits.*)

GRIFFIN. I'm just trying to help the kid.

LARKIN. Oh, you are, are you?

GRIFFIN. Yes, I am. And you know what's got you by the balls, Fr. Larkin? He's doing *better* and you said it couldn't be done.

LARKIN. Oh, yeah, he's a lot better, Mr. Griffin. You're making him a lot more sensitive and feeling.

GRIFFIN. *Yes, I am.*

LARKIN. *Yes, you are.* And what happens to him at the end of the year when you toss him back into his mother's apartment? Are you sure you want him more sensitive and feeling going back in there? Or are you taking him with you when you go? You are going next year, aren't you?—'cause you're not the type who ends up here forever, are you? If you can commit to staying as long as Lee needs you, fine by me. But unless you can make that commitment, get him out. *Now!*

GRIFFIN. I can't do it now . . .

LARKIN. *NOW!*

GRIFFIN. *Give me till the end of the semester, for Christ's sake. I can't* just throw him out! Pretend you have some feelings for once. OK?

LARKIN. (*After pause.*) Christmas vacation.

GRIFFIN. Order him out so I can blame it on you.

LARKIN. (After brief pause.) I trust you to do the right thing . . . for the good of the boy.

(GRIFFIN exits.)

ACT I

Scene 10

LARKIN in chapel, addressing a small congregation. MARCO sings a hymn behind.

LARKIN. (*To audience, easily.*) Juan Carlos asked me a question the other day: "Does *God* have feelings?" I consulted the theologians of the church on the subject and they showed a rare unanimity on the point. No. God does not have feelings. (*Feeling Griffin's accusation of his own seeming heartlessness:*) In fact, it is one of God's most *enviable* perfections that he is able to love every one of us—without feeling anything at all. The Lord be with you.

ALL. (*Softly.*) And also with you.

(LARKIN alone in chapel.)

LARKIN. The kids in this school . . . the kids in this school are the only children I will ever have. For a few years, they're mine. And I don't like the way God treats them. God. The creator of the Pleides . . . the Wonderful . . . the Counsellor . . . the Mighty God . . . the Everlasting Father . . . Father? The God, who—in the goodness of his heart—saved Moses' children . . . by killing Pharaoh's children. The God who saved us all . . . by actually killing his only son. If a parent in the neighborhood behaved like that, I'd call a cop. What cop do I call? (*A loud cry in an empty church:*) *I need a better God.* (*After brief pause:*) Technically that's blasphemy . . . which is the most serious of sins . . . and the only one I commit more than once a day. He doesn't like it, he can hit me with a thunderbolt. He might even be doing me a favor because I'm pretty fucking sick of poverty, chastity and obedience at this stage of the game. (*Kneeling:*) Say the prayers for the dead for our children.

(HENRY appears menacingly behind Larkin. LARKIN turns quickly when he hears Henry.)

LARKIN. What do you want?
HENRY. I want to go to confession.
LARKIN. You?
HENRY. Yeah. I know it's not the right time . . .
LARKIN. No, no. this is fine. This is something I've been looking forward to for a long time.
HENRY. What I tell you, you can't tell anybody, right?
LARKIN. That takes some of the fun out of it, but you're right. I can't tell anybody.

HENRY. Or *do* anything?

(LARKIN nods.)

HENRY. OK, I'm ready to start.

LARKIN. You know how to go to confession?

HENRY. Do I know how to go to confession? "Bless me, father, for I have sinned." Fuck you, do I know how to go to confession. Man, you don't give me any credit. (*HENRY starts to leave.*)

LARKIN. (*Putting on a small purple stole.*) OKOKOK. Let's take a moment to place ourselves in the presence of a loving and merciful God.

HENRY. I think I killed somebody.

LARKIN. People usually start with the small stuff and build up.

HENRY. Fuck the small shit.

LARKIN. What were the circumstances?

HENRY. What?

LARKIN. What was it? Was it self defense? Was it robbery?

HENRY. What is this, a church or a police station, man?

LARKIN. Did you stab the guy? Did you shoot him? What?

HENRY. I didn't do nothing. It was the guy I was with.

LARKIN. Who? (*No answer.*) Who were you with? (*No answer.*) What happened?

HENRY. It wasn't our fault, man. We were in this guy's apartment and he came in. He wasn't supposed to come back till later.

LARKIN. He surprised you?

HENRY. Yes.

LARKIN. (*The details of the crime ring a bell in Larkin's head. Hoping he's wrong.*) Henry, did this man get beaten?

HENRY. Yes.

LARKIN. Seriously?

HENRY. (*In pain, remembering.*) Oh, man . . .

LARKIN. (*Still hoping he's wrong.*) Henry . . . do I know this guy you killed?

HENRY. Maybe.

LARKIN. Does he teach at this school?

HENRY. Maybe.

LARKIN. Shit . . . What would you do to keep him alive, Henry?

HENRY. Anything.

LARKIN. Like never steal again?

HENRY. Never.

LARKIN. (*Imposing hands.*) I forgive you your sins in the name of the Father, the Son and the Holy Spirit. Now get out of here.

HENRY. Am I forgiven?

LARKIN. As soon as you return what you took . . .

HENRY. It's all gone, man . . .

LARKIN. . . . or make it up to him some other way.

HENRY. So he's *not* dead?

LARKIN. Critical, Henry, but not dead.

(*School BELL. HENRY starts to leave.*)

LARKIN. How's Tyro these days, Henry?

HENRY. Who said anything about Ty?

LARKIN. Was Ty the guy you were with?

HENRY. Maybe . . .

LARKIN. Stay away from him, Henry.

HENRY. Can't tell me what to do with my friends.

LARKIN. (*Grabbing Henry by his coat.*) *He's not a friend. Henry. Look, you're a long shot and you've made it this far. Don't fuck it up playing night games with Tyro. Cut him loose.* (*Surprised by his own violence, LARKIN releases Henry.*) You're a good kid, Henry.

HENRY. (*Honestly.*) No, I'm not.

(Heavy rap MUSIC.
LARKIN exits.
HENRY joins the other STUDENTS as they enter.)

ACT I

Scene 11

LEE dances to loud MUSIC in Griffin's apartment.

MARCO .

RIGHT NOW SAGA'S IN A DELICATE POSITION.

YOU KNOW WHAT IT'S LIKE TO BE IN A
    TRANSITION –
    HENRY.

IT HURTS TO BE WITH PEOPLE AND IT HURTS TO
    BE ALONE –

THERE'S A NAME FOR THAT FEELING:
    STUDENTS

YEAH! FUCKED AND FAR FROM HOME.

GRIFFIN. Lee, turn that goddamn music off!
FREDDY.
THE QUESTION FOR SAGA IS –
   STUDENTS.
LIVE OR DIE!
   CARLOS.
THE QUESTION FOR THE GRIFFIN. IS –
   STUDENTS.
FIGHT OR FLY.
   MARCO
IF THE GRIFFIN WAS A LION HE'D HAVE TO –
   STUDENTS.
STAY AND FIGHT!
   FREDDY.
BUT THE GRIFFIN'S GOT WINGS HE CAN TAKE A –
   STUDENTS.
NIGHT FLIGHT!
   HENRY.
BUT SAGA CAN'T FLY—HE'S TIED TO A STAKE –
   MARCO
YOU BETTER MAKE THE RIGHT MOVES –
   STUDENTS.
YOU CAN'T AFFORD A MISTAKE.

(GRIFFIN turns the MUSIC off.
STUDENTS freeze—then exit quietly, leaving LEE alone
   with GRIFFIN.
LARKIN observes the scene.)

GRIFFIN. (*Quiet, into the silence.*) For the last time,
you can't come home with me for Christmas.
   LEE. If I can't go with you . . .

GRIFFIN. . . . you can't . . .

LEE. . . . then let me stay here.

(THEY look at each other in silence.

Then GRIFFIN bursts into activity—there are nicely wrapped presents to be given. Several small boxes and an artist's leather portfolio with a large red bow.)

GRIFFIN. Here—this portfolio is for you. Have it filled by the time I get back. And don't just draw Saga. OK, Lee? All the stuff you need for school. Art. Fruit and bottles and landscapes and all that shit.

LEE. I want to come with you.

GRIFFIN. Did you get your family anything for Christmas?

LEE. Why can't I come with you?

GRIFFIN. No? You can give them these. You can say they're from the both of us. And this is for you. Merry Christmas. Now move it.

LEE. Why can't I stay here?

GRIFFIN. Because you're a minor and if something happens to you, I'm responsible.

LEE. You're sending me to the one place where something will happen to me.

GRIFFIN. I was going to buy Tyro some drugs, but I got him a book on the martial arts instead.

LEE. I shouldn't be talking to you anyway. It was your grandmother who invited me for Christmas. I'll call her. *(LEE moves for the phone.)*

GRIFFIN. *(Cutting him off.)* LOOK, YOU'RE NOT MY FAMILY, OK? I've got a lot to work out with my family. You've got a lot to work out with yours. We've both got to go home, Lee.

LEE. I want to go to *your* home.

(GRIFFIN, weakening, turns to Larkin.)

GRIFFIN. Ed, look, it's only a few days . . .

LARKIN. (*Firm.*) He's got to go back sometime, Tom. When you get back from vacation you can help him sort it out.

(GRIFFIN turns back to Lee.)

LEE. *I won't go.*

GRIFFIN. Tell me, how did I take you from underprivileged to spoiled in less than three months? Christ, it was a mistake to ever let you move in.

LEE. That's what Fr. Larkin thinks. You don't believe that.

(GRIFFIN knows Lee is right. GRIFFIN turns again to Larkin.)

GRIFFIN. Ed . . .

LARKIN. Look, trust somebody for once, would you?

GRIFFIN. (*In pain.*) But I don't buy it.

LARKIN. If you bought it, it wouldn't be trust.

(GRIFFIN doesn't know what to do.)

LEE. (*Simply.*) Griff?

GRIFFIN. Yeah?

LEE. Do *you* want me to go?

(Brief pause.
GRIFFIN has nothing to say.
Door BUZZER.)

GRIFFIN. *(Runs to buzzer, speaks to whoever buzzed.)* We'll be right down.

LEE. You didn't even ask who it was . . .

GRIFFIN. *(Rushing.)* Come on.

LEE. Is it a cab for the airport?

GRIFFIN. Look, it's cold down there. Let's not keep them waiting . . .

LEE. *(Realizing with horror.)* Is it my mother?

GRIFFIN. I'll be back in ten days. You can hold out that long . . .

LEE. *(Driving.)* You had *no right* to call her.

GRIFFIN. *(Justifying, bargaining.)* Look, I had a talk with her—a long talk—she promised me that things would be calm over the holidays.

LEE. *(Driving.)* Was she drunk?

GRIFFIN. Would I have believed her if she were drunk?

LEE. *(Driving.)* That's the only time you *can* believe her. You can throw me out of here, but *you can't make me go home*!

GRIFFIN. *I wouldn't send you to any place I thought was dangerous.*

LEE. *(Final.)* I'm NOT going down there.

GRIFFIN. *WHY DON'T YOU DO SOMETHING FOR ME FOR A CHANGE?*

(LEE smashes a small wrapped gift that Griffin had given him.)

GRIFFIN. *(After brief pause.)* Thank God. I thought I was going to have to listen to those fucking tapes for months.

LEE. Everything's a joke to you, isn't it, Mr. Griffin?

GRIFFIN. *(Very strong to Larkin.)* You're *sure* we're doing the right thing?

LARKIN. Yes.

GRIFFIN. Consequences included.

LARKIN. Yes.

GRIFFIN. *(Bedrock, to Lee.)* You can handle them. I know you can, Lee. Lee, *you won the fight.*

LEE. *(Bedrock.)* I won. You're right. I won the fight. You know what it means? It means that Tyro's got to win the next one. And you know what? After the last couple of months with you I'm not sure I can let myself lose any more. So one of us is going to have to die.

GRIFFIN. *(Looking to Larkin.)* Ed...?

(LARKIN has disappeared. GRIFFIN has to handle this on his own.)

LEE. Merry Christmas, Mr. Griffin.

(LEE holds out a present for Griffin—a folded drawing.)

GRIFFIN. *(Opening the drawing.)* Lee, you didn't have to . . .

(GRIFFIN is stunned by the beauty of the drawing.

Silence.)

LEE. He's a new character in Saga.
GRIFFIN. (*Moved.*) A griffin. It's a masterpiece, Lee.
LEE. It's the best thing I've ever done in my whole life.
GRIFFIN. It's beautiful.
LEE. (*Reaching for the drawing.*) No, it isn't finished...
GRIFFIN. Yes, it is. It's perfect just the way it is.
LEE. Close your eyes and I'll finish it.
GRIFFIN. Are you joking?
LEE. How often do I joke? Close your eyes.

(GRIFFIN hands LEE the picture and closes his eyes.
LEE takes a lighter from his pocket and sets fire to the
    picture.
GRIFFIN opens his eyes.)

GRIFFIN. LEE!

(Too late. The paper burns quickly. GRIFFIN can only
    watch it turn to ashes.
Silence.)

LEE. Now it's yours.
GRIFFIN. Thanks.
LEE. I wanted to give you something beautiful . . . and
take it away from you.

ACT I

Scene 12

*Christmas MUSIC. Griffin's home is suggested. GRIFFIN
walks away from LEE who remains center.*

MOTHER/KENDALL. Tom, welcome home.
FATHER/JAMES. Come right on in, Tommy . . .
MOTHER/KENDALL. Now you stop worrying about
that school for a while and have a good time. You've got a
right to have a good time too, doesn't he, John?
FATHER/JAMES. By all means—it's Christmas.

(GRIFFIN looks back to LEE.)

STUDENTS.
SAGA WAS BIG! SAGA WAS BUILT!
SAGA HAD TO ANSWER FOR THE BLOOD THAT
    WAS SPILT!

*(Lee's house suggested.
A horribly distorted CAROL plays.)*

LEE. (Himself/then his mother/then his brother.) I don't
belong here.
What do you mean you don't belong here? This is your
home.
YEAH. WELCOME HOME, LEE.
ALL. MERRY CHRISTMAS.

(LEE in a sharp down LIGHT backing away from his
family; GRIFFIN in the background joining his family.
A tremendous metal CLANK as if a great door were
swinging shut.
BLACKOUT. INTERMISSION.)

ACT II

Scene 1

The STUDENTS sing a stunningly beautiful, delicate Spanish Christmas hymn. LARKIN enters in a pensive mood as the STUDENTS continue to sing softly:)

LARKIN. Basically Christmas is the story of a bizarre teenage pregnancy. The story, properly read, has enough kinky sex and senseless violence to embarrass the Marquis de Sade. And two nights from now I've got to make it all come out sounding like Silent Night. Silent Night? Hell, there's no such thing as a silent night in New York City.

(Sudden rap MUSIC overtakes the hymn. LARKIN exits as the STUDENTS take over:)

STUDENTS.
COME ON, SAGA, YOU BETTER STAY ALERT –
MARCO.
CAUSE EVEN YOUR FRIENDS ARE TRYING TO GET YOU HURT.
HENRY.
HOW COULD SOMEONE WHO'S SUPPOSED TO BE A FRIEND
PUT HIM BACK IN THE HANDS OF THE BARON AGAIN?

CARLOS.

COME ON, SAGA, BETTER MAKE SOME PLANS –
FREDDY.

'CAUSE ALL YOU GOT ARE YOUR EYES AND
YOUR HANDS –
STUDENTS.

TO GET YOU THROUGH THE TRIAL OF FIRE AND
BLOOD –

FIRE BY NIGHT AND BLOOD BY THE FLOOD.
MARCO.

SHOULD YOU STAY, SAGA BOY, SHOULD YOU
TRY TO WIN?

OR SHOULD YOU JUST GIVE UP ON THIS BATTLE
YOU'RE IN?
HENRY.

OR MAYBE BY NOW YOU'RE JUST TOO OUT OF
SHAPE–

SHOULD YOU JUST TRY TO RUN DOWN THE FIRE
ESCAPE?
MARCO.

SEE, THE TRIAL RIGHT HERE IS THE WORST
TRIAL KNOWN:

LOCKED UP WITH YOUR FAMILY SPENDING
CHRISTMAS AT HOME.
STUDENTS.

WE WANT TO WISH YOU A MERRY CHRISTMAS
(*Whispered:*) MERRY CHRISTMAS!

(*LEE will now go through three days and nights with his
family at Christmas.*

LEE will switch from character to character with the speed
of lightning. (L) indicates Lee; (T) is Tyro; (S) is his
mother, Señora; (M) is Maritza, Tyro's girl friend.

STUDENTS—and FACULTY, if desired—should help to
create a dance-like equivalent for the chaos of Lee's
home.

As LEE passes Christmas vacation with his family,
LARKIN will prepare and deliver his Christmas
sermon:)

LEE. (*Arriving home.*) (L) I don't belong here.

(S) What do you mean you don't belong here? This is your
home. Tell the kids about Christmas.

LARKIN. (*Working on his homily.*) Christmas.

LEE. (L) I don't even have a bed here.

(T) I'm sleeping with Maritza now, Lee. You got a
problem with that? You can sleep on the couch. Tell
the kids about . . .

LARKIN.	LEE.
Christmas . . .	. . . is when a baby without a father . . .
. . . is born in a barn . . .	. . . and we celebrate by killing trees.

LEE. (S) Hey, you show some respect to things that are
holy!

(T) You think you funny, Lee? You think you the big man
now?

(L) No, Ty. You think *you* the big man.

(T) You got a question about that?

(L) Yeah, if you're the big man, how come you're still
living with your mother?

(T) I tried, man, but it's hard 'cause I can't get a job till I get a phone and I can't get a phone till I get a job. Fucking phone company, man, it's screwing up my life.

(L) No job—where you get your money from, Ty?

(T) What money, man? I don't have . . .

(L) I see Maritza's wearing a new dress.

(M) Hey, where I get my clothes is none of your business.

(S) You buying her clothes? Before you buy her clothes I want to see some money coming into this house for the rent. . .

(T) *You see—you see who starts it? Is it him or me?*

(S) And you rob me. You think I don't know where the money goes out of my purse? Lee, now I have to sleep with my money in my hands at night. Someday I'm going to call the police on *you,* then you see how you like it.

(A first fight breaks out.)

ALL. Slap. Slap *back*! Hit. Kick kick kick. Knock down.

LEE. (L) Like a dance. I wonder if it's going to be hard to get back into the dance?

(S) Lee! Lee! Lee! Help me!

(L) Into the dance I go. Slam. Slam. Slam Dance.

STUDENTS. SA - GA! SA - GA! SA - GA!

LEE. (*Rejecting Saga as Griffin advised him.*) NO! I WILL NOT DISAPPEAR INTO SAGA!

FIGHT—KICK—BLEED—ACHE

I WILL NOT BE SAGA. I WON'T TRY TO ESCAPE.

(Night.
The sounds of sleeping.
STUDENTS collapse into sleep around Lee. In sleep, they
become one breathing mass of family weighing on Lee,
trying to claim him.)

LEE. (*Separating himself from the family.*) They sleep.
Let them sleep. I won't shut my eyes. I will draw. I will do
my portfolio. But not what I see. (*LEE breaks free and
draws.*) No, I will dream. I will imagine impossible things.
I will pretend I can see fruit. Fruit on a table. With a table
cloth and a candle. I will pretend that fruit is real. Oranges.
I will draw bottles. I will make up trees. I will imagine
morning.

LARKIN. And then there's the little matter of the
BLOOD! As the innocents are butchered. A perfect feast for
the whole family. Christmas!

*(MORNING—the apartment. TYRO on the prowl; Señora
still in bed.)*

LEE. (T) I could of been an artist too. I could of gone
to Art and Design.
(S) You know, Tyro, there are times I wish you'd go back
to heroin. At least with heroin, you'd get tired and we'd
all get some sleep.
(T) Shut up!
ALL. SLAP!

(A second, more violent fight.)

LEE. (S) LEE! LEE! LEE. Get your brother off me!
Lee! Is that what they teach you in that school—not to
help your mother?
(L) YOU'RE HIS MOTHER, TOO!
ALL. Slap. Hit. Kick. Kick. Kick.

LEE. YOU FIGHT HER BECAUSE SHE'S THE
ONLY ONE YOU CAN BEAT! THEY LAUGH AT YOU
IN THE STREET! YOU TAKE DRUGS SO YOU DON'T
HAVE TO HEAR THEM LAUGHING.

ALL. SLAP. HIT. HIT.

LEE. YOU BUY GUNS BECAUSE YOU DON'T
THINK MARITZA LIKES IT WHEN YOU DO IT TO
HER.

ALL. SLAP. HIT. SLAP. HIT. HIT. HIT.

LEE. COME ON AND HIT ME HARDER BECAUSE
I DON'T WANT TO SAY THESE THINGS. KNOCK ME
OUT BECAUSE I DON'T WANT TO KNOW THESE
THING. YOU ARE ALWAYS GOING TO BE MY
BROTHER! YOU ARE ALWAYS GOING TO BE MY
MOTHER!

*(NIGHT. Again, the family collapses in sleep—intertwined
bodies on a bed. TYRO and LEE speak quietly:)*

LEE. (T) Lee, I can't sleep.
(L) You think that's a secret?
(T) Hold me, Lee.
(L) You got Maritza for that now.
(T) Hold me.

(BROTHER holds BROTHER.)

(L) I don't want to be here.

(T) So go.

(L) I got no place to . . .

(T) Me neither. That's what it means to be a family. Hold me, Lee. Tell me the story.

(L) Christmas is when a baby without a father is born in a barn and . . .

(ALL but LEE sleep.)

LEE. . . . we lie in bed and it's nice and it's sick and it's warm and the kids climb out from under the bed and on top of us and they sleep and she says: Lee, if you run away, take me with you. And I think, if you're still with me, I haven't run away at all. And they all whisper, "Take me with you, take me with you, with you, with you." But I won't sleep. Move. No sleep. I've slept before. I have to see it all. (*LEE removes himself from the group to do as Griffin asked—work on the portfolio.*) I get my portfolio from where I hid it and I draw. I will do what Mr. Griffin says. When they sleep they are all one animal with many souls.

(The FAMILY tries to reclaim Lee. HE resists.)

LEE. No, I don't draw that. My mother is a graceful curve. She is my child and the children are old. No, don't draw that. Oranges. *Apples. Apples.*

(BELLS! BELLS! BELLS! Christmas Eve. A party at Lee's house.)

(S) Dance! Dance! Dance! It's Christmas! Someone dance
    with me! Maritza's dancing. Oh! Lee dances so good!
    Dance, dance, dance!

*(TYRO enters to start the most violent of the fights. It
starts quietly, intensely.)*

(T) Get the fuck away from her.

(M) Come on, Tyro. Dance with me.

(T) No, I'm not going to dance with you. You like to dance
    with Lee. *Dance with Lee then.*

(M) If that's the way you're going to be, I don't want to
    dance at all. I'm going.

(T) You go when I say you go.

(M) You don't own me.

(S) Come on, kids. It's Christmas.

(T) You shut up. This is between me and her.

(L) Oh, so this is how it's going to start.

(A sudden escalation of the violence by TYRO.)

(T) COME ON, LEE. YOU DANCED BEFORE. YOU
    DANCE NOW.

(L) NO!

(T) YOU WANT TO DANCE! DANCE WITH ME!

(L) NOOOO!

(T) COME ON, LEE. YOU WANT TO DANCE, BOY.
    DANCE WITH ME!!!

(L) NOOO! YOU ARE ALWAYS GOING TO BE MY
    BROTHER—YOU ARE ALWAYS GOING TO BE
    MY MOTHER AND I WILL NOT MOVE! I WILL
    SEE WHAT IS HERE! I WILL NOT CHANGE IT!

(Out of the whirl of the violent dance, silence:)

(L) Suddenly it's perfectly quiet. Am I dead? They have stopped. They can't go on. Why? *(A realization starts here that will grow and grow till the end of the monologue:)* If it goes any further he kills her. WELL, GOOD! KILL HER! GET WHAT YOU WANT! I'M NOT GOING TO STOP YOU ANY MORE! *(Silence again:)* I don't stop it, but it stops by itself.

(LARKIN, fully vested for midnight mass, has appeared immediately behind Lee. LARKIN preaches his Christmas homily, building in intensity as LEE's realization grows in fullness:)

LARKIN. Christmas is a hard feast to celebrate . . .
LEE. If I don't stop it, he kills her and the checks stop coming and it's over . . .
LARKIN. It's a feast for children but most of the children in the story are killed . . .
LEE. If I don't stop it, she throws him out and nobody touches her and it's *over*. Jesus Christ! . . .
LARKIN. Why rejoice?
LEE. Jesus Christ, *they don't want it to stop.*
LARKIN. I think I've found a reason.
LEE. And she's crying 'cause she's embarrassed and they're looking at each other like they don't know what to do. It's OK, momi—I'll tell you the story.

LARKIN.
Because amid all the
nightmares . . .

LEE.

I don't know if it will
help . . .

. . . the strange
conceptions . . .

. . . because it's really a
sad story . . .

. . . the murderous
kings . . .

. . . because the king
wants to kill the baby. . .

. . . the bloodshed . . .

. . . but he doesn't
know which baby to to kill
. . .

. . . and the madness . .
.

so he kills all the babies
. . .

. . . there is some good
news!

But you know what
makes it Christmas?

The thing that makes it
Christmas . . .

*YOU KNOW WHAT
MAKES IT
CHRISTMAS?*

One baby gets out!

> *ONE BABY GETS*
> *OUT! MERRY*
> *CHRISTMAS!*

(Wild BELLS!)

LARKIN. *(Joyous.) MERRY CHRISTMAS!*
LEE. *(Wild.) MERRY CHRISTMAS! MERRY CHRISTMAS! MERRY CHRISTMAS! MERRY CHRISTMAS!*

ACT II

Scene 2

The RAP builds into a wild and violent ritual dance celebrating Lee's escape from his family into the streets.

MARCO.
SO THAT WAS IT. THE END OF THE BOUT.
THERE WAS NOTHING MORE TO SAY, SO SAGA WALKED OUT.
HENRY.
JUST LIKE BEFORE HE HAD NO PLACE TO GO
BUT IT WAS BETTER THIS TIME—HE KNEW WHAT HE HAD TO KNOW.
MARCO.
HE KNEW HE WAS THE ONLY ONE WHO WANTED HIM ALIVE

AND HE KNEW WHAT HE HAD TO DO IN ORDER
TO SURVIVE.
HENRY.
A VOICE IN HIS HEAD JUST THE SIZE OF A SEED
SAID:
YOU KNOW WHAT YOU NEED?
STUDENTS.
YOU NEED NOT TO NEED.
MARCO.
I DON'T NEED MY FAMILY –
STUDENTS.
MY FAMILY'S MADE OF STRANGERS!
MARCO.
I DON'T NEED MY FRIENDS –
STUDENTS.
FRIENDS JUST BECOME BETRAYERS!
MARCO.
I DON'T NEED FOOD –
STUDENTS.
FOOD'LL ONLY MAKE YOU FAT!
MARCO.
I DON'T NEED SLEEP –
STUDENTS.
I CAN LIVE WITHOUT THAT!
MARCO.
IF I CAN JUST STAY ALONE THERE IS NO ONE
WHO CAN TELL ME
WHAT TO DO, WHERE TO GO—THEY CAN'T BUY
ME OR SELL ME.
HENRY.
HE'D BE ALL RIGHT AS LONG AS HE COULD STAY
AWAKE.

WITH HIS EYES WIDE OPEN, NOTHING HE
    COULDN'T TAKE.
    MARCO.
HE STAYED AWAKE –
    STUDENTS.
AN HOUR!
    MARCO.
HE STAYED AWAKE –
    STUDENTS.
A DAY!
    MARCO.
HE STAYED AWAKE –
    STUDENTS.
A NIGHT!
    MARCO.
AND HE STARTED TO SAY:
    STUDENTS.
I DON'T NEED MY FAMILY.

(Dance break: the exorcism of the family from Lee.)

    MARCO.
I DON'T NEED MY FAMILY!
    STUDENTS.
MY FAMILY'S MADE OF STRANGERS!
    MARCO.
I DON'T NEED MY FRIENDS!
    STUDENTS.
FRIENDS JUST BECOME BETRAYERS!
    MARCO.
I DON'T NEED FOOD!

STUDENTS.
FOOD'LL ONLY MAKE YOU FAT!
MARCO.
I DON'T NEED SLEEP!
STUDENTS.
I CAN LIVE WITHOUT THAT!
I CAN LIVE WITHOUT THAT!
I CAN LIVE WITHOUT THAT!
I CAN LIVE WITHOUT THAT!
I CAN LIVE WITHOUT THAT!

(The celebration ends in triumph.
Beat.
Sustained school BELL.)

ACT II

Scene 3

*STUDENTS scatter and create a feeling of the first day of
    the second semester.*
*GRIFFIN enters from Christmas, looking fresh and well
    rested.*

GRIFFIN *(Embracing Lee.)* God, it's good to see you,
Lee. I thought about you every day. How was Christmas,
Lee? See, I told you you'd make it through.

(No response from LEE.)

GRIFFIN. My grandmother sent you this. It's only a dollar, but she's old. She thinks it's like twenty.

LEE. (*Avoiding Griffin.*) She's the only one who says Saga's ugly.

GRIFFIN. She didn't mean it. She says anything.

LEE. (*Smothered rage.*) She's the only one who understands it. The portfolio's different. She'd like the portfolio.

GRIFFIN. You did the portfolio?

LEE. Yeah.

GRIFFIN. *Great.* Can I see it?

LEE. It's at the apartment.

GRIFFIN. Let's go . . .

LEE. I can never go back there.

GRIFFIN. (*Beginning to sense serious trouble.*) What happened?

LEE. (*Confronting Griffin.*) Did you have a nice "vacation," Mr. Griffin?

GRIFFIN. Yeah, I did. Everybody was asking for you . . .

LEE. (*With an edge.*) I mean, did you have a nice vacation *from me,* Mr. Griffin?

GRIFFIN. Lee . . .

LEE. 'Cause, you know, I can't take a vacation from me . . . or from my family, Mr. Griffin.

GRIFFIN. Look, Lee, Mr. Griffin's my father. Call me Tom, OK?

LEE. Tom?

GRIFFIN. Yeah.

LEE. I *hate* you, Tom.

(*School bell. LEE walks away from a stunned GRIFFIN.*)

ACT II

Scene 4

STUDENTS and FACULTY minus JAMES: assembly.

LARKIN. At the start of the second semester, let us pray in gratitude for all the graces of first semester—especially the fact that nobody failed out or got thrown out.

HENRY. *All right!*

LARKIN. Henry, the appropriate response is "Lord, hear our prayer."

ALL. Lord, hear our prayer.

(ALL recite the underlined sections; only LARKIN prays the not-underlined sections.)

LARKIN.
Our Father . . .

ALL and LARKIN. Our Father who must be in heaven because you certainly aren't on the block. Hallowed be thy Spanish surname. Thy kingdom come but my will be done in this school as yours is in heaven. Give us this day our daily lunch program and lead us not into temptation but just near enough to keep it interesting. And deliver them from evil for theirs is the kingdom and the power and the glory. . . if only they could see it. Forever and ever. Amen.

LARKIN. Let us add the rest of our petitions in the silence of our hearts.

(GRIFFIN and LEE in SPOTLIGHTS.)

GRIFFIN. (*A phone call home.*) Yes, I'd like to speak to my father which art in Connecticut, please. TOMMY! Say, Dad, you remember when I told you I hated you? WHICH TIME, TOMMY? Look, Dad . . . IT'S OK, TOM. I KNOW YOU DIDN'T MEAN IT. No, I meant it, Dad. I just didn't mean it to hurt so much . . . and I don't want to hurt you about school next year. DON'T TELL ME YOU'RE NOT . . . No, I *am* going to school next year. I'm repeating the tenth grade. See, I've gotten involved in some third world debt, Dad, and I'll never be able to forgive myself if I walk away before it's paid.

ALL. (*As ASSEMBLY returns to focus.*) Lord, hear our prayer.

LARKIN. And let's especially remember Mr. James and pray for his swift return. Amen.

(No response.)

LARKIN. I said AMEN.

ALL. AMEN.

LARKIN. (*Joining the group.*) OK, gentlemen, we all pretend this is a Catholic school in spite of the fact that we all know the real religion around here is *basketball.*

(A basketball is tossed to LARKIN. The atmosphere becomes informal and playful.)

LARKIN. In view of your excellent academic work in the first semester I have decided to reinstitute an event that

we haven't had at Trinity since I broke three ribs during it
several years ago: the Student-Faculty End-of-Term Tackle
Basketball Tournament.

(STUDENTS cheer.)

    LARKIN. IF—IF AND ONLY IF—*NOBODY* fails out
or gets thrown out by spring. Deal?
    STUDENTS and GRIFFIN. *(Cheering.) Deal*!

*(LARKIN becomes a referee about to toss the basketball
    for a jump ball as STUDENTS and FACULTY gather
    around him.)*

    LARKIN. OK, gentlemen—SECOND SEMESTER!
Exams! It's not what you know it's how you test!
    ALL. Yeah!
    LARKIN. God loves a cheerful achiever!
    ALL. Yeah!
    LARKIN. What doesn't kill you, makes you stronger!
    ALL. Yeah!
    LARKIN. And *then* it kills you!
    ALL. Yeah!
    LARKIN. You could be the first third-world president of
the United States!
    ALL.Yeah!
    LARKIN. SECOND SEMESTER!

*(BELL. LARKIN tosses the ball up. ALL leap for it.
    When the group lands it is in the form of a huddle with
    the faculty acting as coaches rushing instructions to the
    STUDENTS.)*

KENDALL. OK, gentlemen, this time of your life is called *puberty* and you will be going through many changes. *None* of these changes is more important, more vital or more mysterious than . . .

GRIFFIN. . . . the change from arithmetic to algebra. In arithmetic you dealt only with "the known." In algebra you begin for the first time to deal with "the unknown." This lets you deal with the larger questions like . . .

LARKIN. The three great questions upon which all religions are built: Who made the world? What went wrong? What do we do now?

GRIFFIN. Some of you have had some algebra at the Boys' Club Saturday classes and you think you know it all, but some of the questions you've been asking like . . .

KENDALL. Can she get pregnant if we do it standing up?—make me think there is some confusion about the basics. So we will start with the word itself: S - E - . . .

GRIFFIN. . . . X stands for *the unknown*. "The unknown," which in this case is . . .

ACT II

Scene 5

Larkin's office.

LARKIN. Tom, did Lee move back in with you?
GRIFFIN. No.

LARKIN. (*An edge.*) Well, congratulations, Tom. You finally made a difference. You made things worse. In its own way that's quite an accomplishment—I didn't think things could get any worse.

GRIFFIN. What the hell are you talking about? I did exactly what you told me to. I threw him back into his mother's apartment for Christmas.

LARKIN. Well, he's not there now.

GRIFFIN. So—where is he?

LEE. (*Appearing and enjoying himself.*) Fr. Larkin doesn't know . . .

LARKIN. (*Right in.*) I don't know . . .

LEE. (*Right in.*) My mother doesn't know . . .

LARKIN. (*Right in.*) His mother doesn't know. He turns up for school and then he disappears . . .

LEE. I'm changing the story. (*LEE disappears.*)

GRIFFIN. He walked out of his mother's apartment?

LARKIN. Yes.

GRIFFIN. I AM *SO PROUD* OF THAT KID!!!

LARKIN. Proud? Tom, *anything* could happen to that kid— anything. He could get *killed* and, because you let him move into your apartment, you know who would be responsible? *The school!* You think that's *funny,* Tom?

GRIFFIN. (*Charged.*) Well, isn't that what we're supposed to be? Responsible? Isn't that what makes us different? Responsibility? Definition of responsibility. Webster's definition. My personal definition. The only one taking any *real* responsibility around here is *Lee Cortez!* (*GRIFFIN starts to exit.*)

LARKIN. *Where are you going?*

GRIFFIN. I'm going to buy a whore a cup of coffee.

LARKIN. Meaning?

GRIFFIN. *Meaning I'm going to find him.* I'm *not* going to let you write this kid off as a percentage point in the loss column. I'm going to get to the heart of the problem for once.

LARKIN. *OK, call me when you get to Adam and Eve.*

GRIFFIN. Bye.

LARKIN. *You've got a class to teach.*

GRIFFIN. *I'm taking a sick day. Ed.*

LARKIN. *Oh. no, you're not. That's how this whole thing started! I'll handle this the way it SHOULD be handled.*

(School BELL: an interview with Señora.

LEE appears. STUDENTS surround the stage to cheer Señora on and amplify the debate when it gets heated.)

LARKIN. It was good of you to come, Señora. I heard you were sick.

LEE. (*Apologetic, as Lee.*) She had a problem with her inner ear.

LARKIN. Has it cleared up, Señora?

LEE. (*Becoming Señora.*) Yes, but now it's the urinary tract, an infection, a cyst, cancer, who knows?

LARKIN. Did you read the booklet that I sent you?

LEE. (Señora) Lee's doing bad at school?

LARKIN. (*Business-like, rapidly.*) No, but school work isn't the limit of my responsibility to Lee, Señora, and I am beginning to think it might be better for everyone if Lee moved into a home.

LEE. (*Señora–shocked.*) A home?

LARKIN. Yes, a group home, señora.

LEE. (Señora) No!

(Fight BELL.)

HENRY. ROUND ONE!

*(STUDENTS create a sense of a fight arena with an active
crowd around LARKIN's attempt to deal with Señora.)*

LARKIN. He's starting to have a hygiene problem,
señora, he wears the same clothes to school every day . . .

LEE. (Señora) I am not a rich woman . . .

LARKIN. . . . and he talks to no one. No one. Put all
this together, señora, and it's spells "neglect."

STUDENTS. *(Calling the fight.)* Hand!

LARKIN. *(Building.)* . . . and that's a form of "abuse" .
. .

STUDENTS. Slap!

LARKIN. . . . and for abuse you have to notify *Welfare*
. . .

STUDENTS. Fist! Fist! Fist!

LARKIN. *(Machiavelli.)* . . . and rather than putting
your welfare payments in jeopardy, wouldn't it be better to
consider putting Lee in a home?

(Fight BELL.)

CARLOS. First round to Father Larkin!

LEE. *(Señora—rising to leave.)* I looked at the book,
Father. It is a very nice home. Rugs on the floor, very
nice. But my son, he has a home.

STUDENTS. Hand!

LARKIN. But your son hasn't been staying at home.

LEE. (Señora.) Whose fault is that? A teacher stole him from my house.

STUDENTS. Slap!

GRIFFIN. (*Taking over.*) He asked to live with me, Señora, because he was tired of being beaten up. If you cared about him at all you wouldn't let his brother beat him.

LEE. (Señora.) And you never fought with your brothers, Señor?

STUDENTS. Slap!

GRIFFIN. Not to the point of drawing blood.

STUDENTS. Slap back!

LEE. (Señora.) Ah, but you are a white boy, Señor.

STUDENTS. Fist! Fist! Fist!

(Fight BELL.)

HENRY. Round to *Señora.*

(Cheers and ad libs encouraging Señora from the STUDENTS.)

LEE. (Señora) Here is your book back, padre . . .

LARKIN. Please keep the booklet, Señora. Perhaps we can speak again if there is any trouble in the future.

LEE. (*Señora—exiting.*) Muchas gracias, padre.

(Exit STUDENTS.)

GRIFFIN. Wait a minute. That's it? You're going to let her go? We don't know where the kid's sleeping at night.

LARKIN. (*Last word on the subject.*) Look, it's her kid, all right? All we can do is wait for the next crisis.

GRIFFIN. OK, Ed. Here's the next crisis. (*Declaring war:*) SEÑORA! YOU'RE AN UNFIT MOTHER!

LARKIN. TOM!

LEE. (*Señora—ready for war herself.*) Tyro will come and speak with you and you will be *very* sorry for speaking to me with no respect.

GRIFFIN. (*Blocking Señora's exit.*) Oh, he's your enforcer—so that's it—I never could figure out why you kept him and threw out Lee.

LEE. (Señora) Lee will find a way. His brother is not so strong.

GRIFFIN. Lady, he's a psychopath! Somebody ought to kick his ass.

LEE. (Señora.) He's my *son*!

GRIFFIN. *Lee's your son, too, and you don't give a shit about him*!

LEE. (Señora.) I love Lee.

GRIFFIN. (*Nasty.*) Right. If you cared *one bit* . . .

LEE. (*Señora—exploding full force.*) *I love my children.*

GRIFFIN. *If you loved him you'd let him move into this home.*

LEE. (Señora.) *I LOVE MY FAMILY AND YOU ARE TEARING IT APART.*

GRIFFIN. *Lady. I'd LOVE to tear your family apart. I just can't find a way to do it.*

LEE. (Señora.) *YOU ARE A BAD MAN! AN EVIL MAN!*

GRIFFIN. (*Over the top.*) *Evil? Lady, I didn't know what evil was before I met your family. I thought it was a sort of mistake that people kept making over and over. It took your family to teach me that it was a taste for something bad.*

LEE. (*Señora.*) *I AM DOING EVERYTHING THAT I CAN DO FOR MY CHILDREN! EVERYTHING!*

GRIFFIN. *WELL, IT'S NOT ENOUGH!*

LARKIN. *TOM!*

LEE. (*Señora—crying out in pain and fury.*) *ASK LEE! ASK LEE IF HE WANTS TO GO TO THIS "HOME." IF HE SAYS YES I WILL SIGN ANY PAPER YOU WANT. BUT HE WON'T DO THAT BECAUSE NO MATTER WHAT YOU THINK OF US—WE ARE STILL HIS FAMILY!*

LARKIN. Señora, would you please step into my office. I don't want you to leave like this.

(LEE exits as Señora.)

GRIFFIN. (*Rapid fire.*) Right! Now you're going to make nice-nice with her and sell me down the drain. "He's a young teacher, señora. He doesn't understand, señora. Please forgive him, señora." *LOOK! I'M NOT THE ONE WHO'S BEATING UP ON HER SON.*

LARKIN. (*Exploding.*) *NO. YOU'RE THE ONE WHO'S BEATING UP ON HER!* First, her husbands. Then her son. Now, you. Congratulations, you've got the hang of the neighborhood real fast. Look, *she* is *not* the problem.

GRIFFIN. (Driving.) Then who is?

LARKIN. (*Hammering at Griffin.*) *YOU*—at the moment! I *order* you to stay away from Lee's family before you do some real harm. If you have to get it out of your

system, go down to the gym and put on a pair of gloves, but, for Christ's sake, *pick on someone who can hit back!*
GRIFFIN. (*An idea dawning.*) I will!

(*LARKIN moves to a removed area of the stage.*
LEE leaps onto stage as Tyro; GRIFFIN pounds on the apartment door; STUDENTS appear again to provide sound and an atmosphere of violence for the coming fight between Tyro and Griffin.)

GRIFFIN. OPEN THE DOOR! OPEN THE DOOR!

LEE. (Tyro) Lee's not here!

GRIFFIN. I'm not here for Lee. I want to see *you.*

LEE. (Tyro) I don't want to see you, you faggot.

GRIFFIN. Faggot? Faggot? That's the worst word you can come up with, faggot? There are a lot of worse words than faggot.

LEE. (Tyro) Not on this block.

GRIFFIN. What about words like "asshole"? You know, the kind of words that apply to you.

LEE. (Tyro) Fuck you.

GRIFFIN. Fuck you.

LEE. (Tyro) Fuck you.

GRIFFIN. Fuck you.

LARKIN. *Never let the student set the tone of the discussion.*

GRIFFIN. (*Slamming the door.*) Open this door! What? You afraid of the white-boy, you latino macho asshole!

LEE. (Tyro) GET THE FUCK OUT OF HERE. I'M WARNING YOU!

GRIFFIN. OK, I'M WARNED. NOW OPEN THE FUCKING DOOR! (*GRIFFIN smashes through the door.*) Hi, there, Tyro. How the hell are you?

LEE. (*Tyro—pinned by GRIFFIN.*) STOP IT. STOP IT, MAN!

GRIFFIN. Don't "maaaaaan" me, Tyro, like the cool dudes do, 'cause if you were a cool dude you'd be rich or dead by now.

LEE. (Tyro) What the fuck do you want?

GRIFFIN. (*Beating up Tyro.*) I want to beat the shit out of you because I'm sick and tired of fucking around with you third-hand. Now you leave your mother and Lee alone or I'll throw you off the roof of this building.

LEE. (Tyro) BACK OFF, MAN.

GRIFFIN. I told you, don't "maaaaan" me, asshole. People who beat up on women don't get to use that word.

LEE. (Tyro) You don't know shit.

GRIFFIN. Yes, I do. I do know shit cause I know *you.*

(*TYRO breaks away from Griffin. STUDENTS disappear.*)

LEE. (Tyro) Man, I'm made of the same stuff as Lee. You think that's shit?

GRIFFIN. You leave Lee out of this.

LEE. (Tyro) I haven't even seen him since you started sucking him off.

GRIFFIN. You shut up.

LEE. (Tyro) Truth hurts, huh, man?

GRIFFIN. The truth is fine. You know what the truth is? There is a problem here and the problem is *you.*

LEE. (*Tyro—taking over.*) I'm the problem—Well, that ought to make things easy then. Get rid of me an everything'll be all right—my mother won't drink any more and the apartment'll be Trump-fucking-Tower, right? *Call the mayor, man. The teacher knows what the problem is! ME! I'm the problem, man.*

GRIFFIN. I told you —don't "MAN" me, maaaaaan.

LEE. (Tyro) *LOOK—CUT THIS "MAAAAAN"-SHIT, YOU ASSHOLE! WHITE BOYS DON'T GET TO MAKE THE RULES DOWN HERE ON WHO'S A MAN, OK?*

GRIFFIN. (*Acknowledging Tyro's point.*) OK. Talk . . . and we'll see what you have to say.

LEE. (*Tyro—vastly amused.*) We'll? *We'll?* Who's *WE*, man? You got somebody in the hall waiting for you? We? You scared to talk with me by yourself, man?

GRIFFIN. (*An honest offer.*) *Talk.* I'll listen . . . I'll try to understand.

LEE. (*Stepping out of Tyro.*) Listen, Mr. Griffin, but *don't* understand.

LARKIN. (*Delicately.*) Teach, just teach.

(With a CRASH, GRIFFIN and LEE merge as Tyro. THEY will both speak as Tyro, occasionally speaking for themselves. BOTH stay constantly on the move with the heightened energy that comes from Ty's swagger, anger and revelations.
Over the course of the scene, GRIFFIN gets deeply inside Tyro—allowing LEE the freedom to step out.)

LEE and GRIFFIN. (*Tyro—exploding.*) Yeah, there's a problem here, man, but it isn't me. I am doing all I can. This is my life. This is MY LIFE, man, and I'm *living* it! Are you listening to me?

GRIFFIN. (As Griffin.) I'm listening.

LEE. (As Lee.) Don't.

LEE. (Tyro) I'll tell you something about your life, man. You don't come down here for Lee or for anybody else. You come down here because you look around at college and you say to yourself . . .

GRIFFIN and LEE. (Tyro) "Shit, man, this can't be *my life!*"

GRIFFIN. (Tyro) So you come down here to find out what's going on in the streets. You come down here to watch people like me *live* and then you take stories back to your friends at parties on high floors of white buildings.

GRIFFIN and LEE. (Tyro) You talk about me to your friends?

LEE. (As Lee) Tell him no.

GRIFFIN. (as Griffin.) Yes.

GRIFFIN. (Tyro) And they all think . . .

GRIFFIN and LEE. (Tyro) "What a nice guy he is! What a good white boy!"

GRIFFIN. (Tyro) Man, *white people!* They live scared shitless they're going to fail out of some school and they die thinking . . .

GRIFFIN and LEE. (Tyro) "Jesus, I hope they all know what a nice boy I been."

GRIFFIN. (Tyro) But your friends, they take one look at me and they think . . .

GRIFFIN and LEE. (Tyro) "Call a cop."

GRIFFIN. (Tyro) That's 'cause I'm no school boy.

GRIFFIN and LEE. (Tyro) I am a man.

GRIFFIN. (As Griffin.) Look, all I'm trying to do is to help Lee.

GRIFFIN and LEE. (Tyro) Fuck Lee!

GRIFFIN (As Griffin.) He's got a lot of talent . . .

GRIFFIN and LEE. (Tyro) *Lee's* got talent? WHAT
ABOUT *ME*, MAN? WHAT ABOUT *ME*?

GRIFFIN. (As Griffin.) Look, I'll help you . . .

GRIFFIN. (*Tyro, then himself.*) Help me *what*, man?
I'll help you get back into school.

GRIFFIN and LEE. (Tyro) *School*? *Shit!*

GRIFFIN. (*Tyro, then himself.*) I graduated, man. I
thought you got thrown out.

GRIFFIN and LEE. (Tyro) I graduated!

LEE. (Tyro) I didn't wait for nobody's permission to
graduate.

GRIFFIN. (Tyro) I left when I was ready . . .

LEE. (Tyro) . . . not when fucking Fr. Larkin told me I
was ready.

GRIFFIN. (Tyro) As long as you still need somebody
to tell you when you finished with school . . .

GRIFFIN and LEE. (Tyro) . . . you still a boy—and
you're still a boy . . .

GRIFFIN. (Tyro) . . . aren't you . . .

GRIFFIN and LEE. (Tyro) . . . white boy?

(LEE steps out of Ty and watches Griffin.
GRIFFIN descends into the depths of Tyro step by step to
the core of sorrow and pain:)

GRIFFIN. (*Tyro/Griffin alternating.*) You going back
to school? Yes. Not me, man, I graduated . . . I can't go
back . . . This is my life. I could help you get back in . . .
For what? (*Slowing down some. Deeper and deeper into
Ty's pain.*) What am I gonna be, man? A doctor? . . . A
lawyer? . . . Man, doctors don't come from Rivington
Street. Waiters do. Lawyers don't live on Avenue D and

Third . . . If I'm successful, I mean if I'm really successful,
you know what job I get? . . . Security guard. Security
guard, man. Big—fucking—deal . . . Shit, it makes me
mad.

*(Sound of GLASS breaking as TYRO punches out the
windows in his apartment.*
*On the first punch, Ty is played by GRIFFIN and LEE.
THEY are then joined by the STUDENTS-as-Ty for the
remaining punches as GRIFFIN becomes himself
again.)*

GRIFFIN, LEE and STUDENTS. (*A karate punch and
shout.*) HUH! Shit, I cut my fucking hand. Now you see
what you made me do?

GRIFFIN. (*With abandon.*) You go ahead, Ty. Punch
out the windows.

LEE and STUDENTS. (*Punching.*) HUH!

GRIFFIN. Punch them *all* out cause when you're done
we've got some work to do.

STUDENTS. (*Punching.*) HUH!

LEE. (*Becoming Señora.*) Señor, is *this* your idea of
helping my family? Even on the worst day of my life, my
apartment never looked this bad.

STUDENTS. (*Punching.*) HUH!

GRIFFIN. (*Rapid fire.*) Señora, if I can do something
for Tyro, will you sign the papers for Lee?

STUDENTS. (*Punch.*) HUH!

GRIFFIN/LEE. (*Señora—rapid fire throughout.*) Oh no!
OH NO!

LEE. (Señora) You take away what's best and leave me
with what's bad?

GRIFFIN. (Señora) The day they killed my father . . .

LEE. (Señora) . . . they shot him two times in the back of the head in his store on Essex . . .

GRIFFIN. (Señora) . . . I came home from the funeral . . .

LEE. (Señora) . . . one friend of mine just stabbed another in the hallway . . .

GRIFFIN/LEE. (Señora) I wore *black* for a long time that year . . .

LEE. (Señora) Too many people take away too much from me . . .

GRIFFIN. (Señora.) And now you want to take away my *good* boy and leave me with *Tyro*? Oh, no!

STUDENTS. (*Punch.*) HUH!

GRIFFIN. (*As Griffin—roaring forward.*) Look, if I can do something for Tyro, will you sign the papers?

LEE. (Señora) Sometimes I think no one can do anything for Tyro . . .

GRIFFIN. But if I can . . .

LEE. (Señora) Sometimes I think God himself cannot do anything for Tyro . . .

GRIFFIN. BUT IF I CAN, *WILL YOU SIGN THE PAPERS*?

GRIFFIN/LEE. (Señora) Yes.

LEE. (Señora) No.

GRIFFIN/LEE. (Señora) Yes.

GRIFFIN. (Handshake.) *Deal!*

STUDENTS. (*Final punch.*) HUH!

LEE. (*Señora—with a touch.*) Welcome to the family, Tomas!

(School BELL.)

ACT II

Scene 6

*School BELL: enter LARKIN, KENDALL and JAMES. A
second semester teachers' meeting.
GRIFFIN remains preoccupied with his encounter with
Tyro.*

LARKIN. (*To Griffin.*) Welcome back, Tom. Where the
hell have you been for the last three periods? (*Convening
the meeting:*) The first order of business is to welcome Mr.
Mitchell James back. I think I speak for the whole faculty
when I say that your absence was . . . noticed.

JAMES. (*Cheerfully nasty.*) Thank you very much,
father. None of you so much as dropped me a card while I
was in the hospital. So much for Christian charity.

KENDALL (*Matching him.*) My sentiments exactly.
Did the students all tell you that they wished you'd died?

JAMES. Yes, as a matter of fact, they did. Thank you
very much, Mr. Kendall.

KENDALL You're welcome, Mr. James.

LARKIN. Second item—any students to be discussed?

(JAMES' hand flies into the air.)

LARKIN. The chair recognizes Mr. James.

JAMES. Henry Rodriguez.

KENDALL Shit.

(HENRY appears at the center of the scene.)

JAMES. I overheard a spelling bee in Mr. Kendall's classroom this morning . . .

KENDALL. I can explain . . .

JAMES. The most extraordinary words were being used . . .

JAMES.	HENRY. *(Delighted with himself.)*
Henry, in particular, was dealing with a specialized vocabulary . . .	
	. . . Diaphragm . . .
. . . well above his years . . .	
	. . . Prophylactic . . .
. . . multi-syllabic . . .	
	. . . Menstruation . . .
. . . even foreign words . . .	
	. . . Fellatio . . .
. . . and he was handling even the most advanced work . . .	
	. . . Coitus.

JAMES. . . . with great skill and maturity. *(With simple sincerity:)* I think Mr. Kendall is to be commended.

(A new MITCHELL JAMES has appeared. KENDALL searches for an explanation.)

KENDALL. (*After a pause.*) Mitchell, are you on medication?

JAMES. No.

KENDALL. Well, then—thank you, Mitch.

JAMES. You're welcome, Burke.

LARKIN. (*As HENRY disappears.*) Any other students?

GRIFFIN. (*Darkly.*) Yes . . . Tyro Cortez.

JAMES. Now there's a name we haven't heard in a while.

GRIFFIN. You were wrong to throw him out of here, Ed.

LARKIN. I told you to stay away from him.

GRIFFIN. He's the heart of the problem, isn't he, Ed?

LARKIN. (*Bulldozing forward.*) Next order of business—scheduling. Burke, test schedule, please.

KENDALL. (*Rapid fire.*) The first round of public school tests hits at the end of the month—then the Specialties (Bronx Science and Art and Design). Oh, Tom, the Art and Design portfolios are due the day of the exam . . .

GRIFFIN. Why are you telling me?

KENDALL. Just thought you'd like to know. Then, the ever popular, week-long CTBS—that's the Comprehensive Test of Basic Skill to the Uninitiated.

GRIFFIN. Why lose a whole week of teaching?

KENDALL. Because that's how long they take.

GRIFFIN. Then why give them?

KENDALL. (*Clever, but true.*) Because somebody has to be the bottom ten percent on standardized tests and if our kids don't do it the people on Staten Island will be very upset.

GRIFFIN. It all looks pretty funny after a while, doesn't it, Burke?

KENDALL. Ed . . .

GRIFFIN. No, I think it's funny too.

KENDALL. (*On the attack.*) Look, you object to my having a sense of humor? You try living with the apocalypse as long as I have without one.

JAMES. (*The new MITCHELL JAMES.*) No, let's listen to him. Maybe he has a point. Maybe we are too callous.

GRIFFIN. (*After brief pause.*) Mitch, please don't agree with me. I can't take it. I need somebody to be consistently an asshole around here, Mitch, and, Mitch, I was sort of counting on you.

KENDALL. (*Attack intensifies.*) That's right. *We're* funny—the kids *aren't*.

LARKIN. Burke is right.

GRIFFIN. (*Gauntlet thrown.*) *Tyro Cortez is dying*!

KENDALL. (*Taken up.*) Tyro? Ty? . . . Oscar Menendez. Phillipe Moscea. Jose Escobar. We've all been through it, Tom.

JAMES. Ramon Peralta. Paul Matteo. Alex Sanchez...

KENDALL. (*Powerful last word on the subject.*) It's a *long* list and we've fought for *all* of them but sometimes the damage is just too deep. So as for this "I'm in more pain than you" pedagogical adolescence you're selling—it's a *phase. Get through it.*

GRIFFIN. (*From the center of the earth.*) To where? To a city full of kids on your MIA list, Burke? To a city where we start treating violence like a natural disaster? NO, it's an *UN*natural disaster and you all know it or you wouldn't be here. You need something better than one more person adding names to your list. I may not be it. I'm sorry for that. You deserve better. But I'm your best shot. And I will *NOT* add *ONE MORE NAME* to that list.

LARKIN. (*After brief pause, rapid-fire.*) Look, you think you've got to save Ty—this has nothing to do with me. But I don't want him in here 'cause I already fought that battle once and lost. And I expect you to be here and *brilliantly* prepared every day because there is a whole school full of kids that I am trying to save and I won't have them sacrificed for one boy who is already dead.

GRIFFIN. (*Matching Larkin.*) I am not giving up on Tyro any more than I'm giving up on Lee.

JAMES. (*Easy—breaking the drive.*) Actually Lee seems much improved to me.

GRIFFIN. Well, it has nothing to do with me. He won't even *talk* to me.

KENDALL. Don't take all the credit. He won't speak to any of us.

LARKIN. We don't even know where he's living.

JAMES. He's living in the elevator shack on the top of Marco Ruiz's building.

(*Dead stop.*)

GRIFFIN. *What?*

JAMES. He's living in the elevator shack on the top of Marco Ruiz's . . .

GRIFFIN. (*Shock.*) He told *you* that?

JAMES. I didn't realize that it was any big deal.

LARKIN. It is.

JAMES. Then I can't imagine why he chose to tell me. He and I have never been close.

LARKIN. (*Praising James to cut Griffin.*) You never know how a teacher can touch a student's life. Maybe it was something you said *in class*. Congratulations, *Mitch*.

(*TEACHERS exit. LEE appears instantaneously. The roof.*)

GRIFFIN. Why did you tell Mr. James?

LEE. Because I knew it would hurt you. I was going to tell Fr. Larkin, but I told Mr. James because I knew it would hurt you more. I told him it was a secret so he'd tell you right away . . . Did it hurt you, Griff? You feel left out?

GRIFFIN. Yes.

LEE. Not as left out as I felt at Christmas.

GRIFFIN. I went to confession about that, but God couldn't forgive me only you can. Forgive me?

LEE. I like being more powerful than God.

GRIFFIN. See you around then.

LEE. (*Stopping GRIFFIN's exit with a question.*) You fought with my brother?

GRIFFIN. Who told you?

LEE. I can see into the apartment from here. I can see everything they do. I don't need to hear them. I hear them in my head all the time. Before I moved in with you I thought that was just the way the world sounded . . . You were fighting about me?

GRIFFIN. Yeah.

LEE. Who won?

GRIFFIN. I did.

LEE. I can fight my own battles.

GRIFFIN. I know that. Hell, you're more powerful than God . . . Mr. Kendall wants you to know the Art and Design interview's coming up. You need anything for it?

LEE. Get my portfolio?

GRIFFIN. Why not get it yourself?

LEE. I can't go back there.

GRIFFIN. Why not leave them for good?

LEE. I don't know, Griff; why don't you leave me?

GRIFFIN. Because you're like a brother.

LEE. He *is* my brother.

GRIFFIN. Yeah, well . . . (*GRIFFIN starts to exit.*)

LEE. (*Stopping him with a word.*) Tom? . . . Tom, I'm glad you came looking for me. I didn't know if you would.

GRIFFIN. I'll always come looking for you, Lee.

LEE. Thanks.

GRIFFIN. (*Older brother.*) Lee, if your mother signs those papers Fr. Larkin gave her, you're going to have to go to that home.

LEE. She'll never sign.

GRIFFIN. You never know.

LEE. Griff, some things don't change. Your family's your fate.

GRIFFIN. (*Losing patience badly.*) Oh, enough. Enough! *Shit* on *Saga.*

LEE. Saga knows what he's talking about.

GRIFFIN. He's a jerk if he thinks things can't change. Your brother doesn't think that way. He's willing to change.

LEE. He told you that?

GRIFFIN. (*Bragging.*) *Yes.*

(*After brief pause:*)

LEE. (*Amazed.*) And you *believed* him?

GRIFFIN. Yeah, I know what your brother needs.

LEE. (*Simple truth.*) You don't know nothing, Griff. You don't even know who won the fight. (*LEE exits.*)

GRIFFIN. (*Furious at having his victory turn hollow.*) I won the fight. *I did. I won the fight! And your mother's going to sign those papers! And YOU'RE GOING TO THAT HOME!*

(*Insistent school BELL.*)

ACT II

Scene 7

School BELL: Suddenly GRIFFIN is in the middle of a school day involving all STUDENTS and FACULTY. LARKIN appears on balcony.

LARKIN. Mr. Griffin!

GRIFFIN. Yes, Father.

LARKIN. Would you mind if I observed your class this period?

GRIFFIN. Mind? Mi. . . ? No, *not at all.*

(*School BELL. LARKIN moves across the set to Griffin's classroom.*)

GRIFFIN. (*To the world.*) DOES ANYBODY KNOW WHAT I'M SUPPOSED TO BE TEACHING THIS PERIOD?

ALL. (*Except LARKIN.*) SCIENCE!

(*FACULTY exits, leaving GRIFFIN with his class.*)

GRIFFIN. That's right. Science. Today we'll do a description of the atom.

HENRY. We did that yesterday.

GRIFFIN. Look, Henry, Fr. Larkin's going to be observing me today, so don't bust my chops for once, OK?

LARKIN. (*Arriving at the classroom.*) Mr. Griffin, may I...?

GRIFFIN. (*Indicating a seat.*) Certainly. OK, class, today we're going to study the atom. Now the atom . . .

HENRY. (*For Larkin's benefit.*) Mr. Griffin?

GRIFFIN. Yes, Henry.

HENRY Mr. Griffin, did you correct our homework last night?

GRIFFIN. (*No.*) Yes, Henry, I did. Now, the atom . . .

HENRY Are you going to pass it back?

GRIFFIN. (*No.*) Yes, Henry, I am, but NOT right now. If you want, you can get it from me *AFTER SCHOOL*?

HENRY That's all right.

(*In the context of Griffin's class, we will now follow GRIFFIN on a journey through several weeks of his life and the life of Lee's family.*

There are too many changes of place and time to note them all, but major changes are noted. All changes should be as close to instantaneous as possible. STUDENTS,

LIGHTS, and SOUND help throughout to define the sense of each place.)

GRIFFIN. Now, the atom. There was a time when people thought the entire universe was made of earth, air, fire and water. We have discovered, however, that these elements are made up of particles and these particles are electrically charged. They pull and they push on each other. *None of them just lies around on the fucking couch all day.*

(Apartment.)

STUDENTS. GRIFFIN, GRIFFIN.

GRIFFIN. *(Tyro, himself.)* WELL, WHAT DO YOU WANT ME TO DO? I want you to see a psychiatrist. FUCK PSYCHIATRISTS. No, I think they charge extra for that. MAN, I SEEN THE PSYCHIATRIST IN EVERY SCHOOL I EVER BEEN TO. LET ME TELL YOU SOMETHING—IF THEY TELL YOU TO DRAW A PICTURE OF YOUR FAMILY, DRAW THE SAME NUMBER OF FINGERS ON EVERYBODY OR THEY GET REAL UPSET.

STUDENTS. HUH!

GRIFFIN. OK, reality therapy then. You're getting a job!

(School BELL: Classroom.)

GRIFFIN. Any questions?
STUDENTS. HUH!

(Rooftop.)

LEE. Yes. Did you get my portfolio?

GRIFFIN. Goddamn it, I forgot.

LEE. "Forgot?" That's a second grade sort of an excuse for a teacher to be using, isn't it?

STUDENTS. HUH!

(Apartment.)

GRIFFIN. *Where's the portfolio, Ty?*

LEE. (Tyro) He does beautiful work, man . . .

GRIFFIN. . . . and you're made of the same stuff as he is, Ty. Fr. Larkin says . . .

GRIFFIN and LEE. (Tyro) Who the fuck cares what Fr. Larkin says?

LEE. (Tyro) All his stories about the streets . . .

GRIFFIN. (Tyro) When you ever see him in the streets?

LEE. (Tyro) He doesn't know how to help me, man . . .

GRIFFIN. (Tyro) Help me, man.

LEE. (Tyro) Help me, man.

GRIFFIN. *(To Lee.) Help me.*

LEE. *(To Griffin.) Help me!*

(Short BELL: Larkin's office.)

LARKIN. *(Fast.)* Help yourself to some coffee, Tom. About the class, it was good . . .

GRIFFIN. Yeah?

LARKIN. Yeah, but then again, why wouldn't it be— you taught it two days in a row. Gonna keep teaching it till you get it right?

GRIFFIN. (Tyro) So what? So I fuck up—so what?

LARKIN. Who said you were fucking up? You got Lee coming to school.

(Short BELL: Classroom.)

GRIFFIN. *(After short BELL.)* Your report, please, Lee.

LEE. A nuclear explosion is made up of a chain reaction of small explosions—in themselves harmless—but together they can destroy a city.

GRIFFIN. Very good.

LEE. From this we get the expression nuclear family.

(Short BELL: Larkin's office.)

LARKIN. Good work, Lee.

LEE. *(Running off.)* Did you get my portfolio, Griff?

GRIFFIN. *(Ignoring Lee, hammering Larkin.)* Ty's making it, Ed.

LARKIN. *(Heading off to class.)* It's sheer luck, Tom.

GRIFFIN. *Ty's getting it together, Ed.*

LARKIN. Stay away from that family.

GRIFFIN. *Aren't you even going to ask about Ty?*

LARKIN. *(Turning on him.) What do I have to do to get you to hear me?*

GRIFFIN. *(Real need.) Why can't you give me some credit for once?*

STUDENTS. HUH!

(Inside Larkin's thoughts.)

LARKIN. (*Personal and immediate.*) Once we had a runner here so good I kept leaving him back 'cause we needed him to anchor our mile relay. A beautiful boy. Turned out to be a good street runner too. Late one night I caught him taking our computers out for a midnight walk. His parents decided I should press charges—try to shake the kid up. The judge was great. Said all the right things. Gave him a light six months. A month in—he got his throat slit in jail . . . I said the funeral. Since then, two things changed. A. I don't cry at funerals and B. I don't fuck with the ecology. The world's a very unforgiving place, Tom. It just isn't built for kids like Tyro.

GRIFFIN. So what are they—evolutionary mistakes?

(BELL: classes change.)

LARKIN. (*On to class.*) Teach the ones who have a chance.

GRIFFIN. (*Major stand.*) *Ed, I got Tyro a job.*

LARKIN. (*Exiting.*) I believe you have a class.

GRIFFIN. *He's got a job, Ed, and he's doing real well at it.*

LEE. (*Incredible event.*) You really got him a . . .

GRIFFIN. Well, it's not much of a . . .

(Apartment.)

GRIFFIN and LEE. (Tyro) SO I MISSED ONE DAY OF WORK—ONE DAY—*SO WHAT?*

GRIFFIN. (*Pressuring Ty hard.*) You can't *pick* what days you go to work. You go to work *every* . . .

GRIFFIN and LEE. (Tyro) NO, MAN, THAT'S TOO
HARD . . .

GRIFFIN. (*Pressure on.*) Yes, it's hard! That's why they
call it *WORK*, Tyro—That's why they call it *WORK*!

STUDENTS. HUH!

LEE. (Señora) Señor, do you have any idea how much
Tyro makes dealing on the street?

GRIFFIN and LEE. (Señora) How do you expect my
family to EAT, señor, if my son gets a *JOB*!?!

STUDENTS. HUH!

GRIFFIN. *He can do it! He can do it!*

(A health club.)

GRIFFIN and LEE. (Tyro) A health club, man. Fuck it.

LEE. (Tyro) They got all these pictures on the outside
of all these beautiful women and built men.

GRIFFIN. (Tyro) Inside, man, it's like sumo-wrestlers.

GRIFFIN and LEE. (Tyro) Lifeguard?

GRIFFIN. (Tyro) Man, I got whole sports in me that
nobody's ever played . . .

LEE. (Tyro) . . . and I'm a lifeguard at a pool the size of
two bathtubs . . .

GRIFFIN/LEE. (Tyro) . . . watching fat people soak
their assholes.

GRIFFIN. (Tyro) I don't want to guard their lives,
man—

LEE. (Tyro) I want them fucking dead.

GRIFFIN/LEE. (Tyro) That's not a good way for a
lifeguard to feel, man.

STUDENTS. HUH!

(Apartment.)

GRIFFIN. At least you're making it to work, Ty. I'm proud of you. What are you doing with the money?

GRIFFIN and LEE. (Tyro) I bought a gun.

(Dead stop.)

GRIFFIN. (*Quietly —genuinely surprised.*) A gun? Look, Ty, I know you're under a lot of pressure. I know how it feels, but a gun . . .

LEE. (Tyro) NO, YOU DON'T. YOU *DON'T* KNOW HOW IT FEELS! HOW WOULD YOU KNOW HOW IT . . .

GRIFFIN. Then *teach* me! *Teach me* how it feels.

(TYRO knees Griffin.)

GRIFFIN. JESUS CHRIST, TY!

LEE. (*Tyro—with a choke hold on Griffin as all STUDENTS watch.*) Relax.

GRIFFIN. (*Struggling for breath.*) Ty . . .

LEE. (*Tyro—tightening hold.*) Relax . . . How you feel, man? Your heart going fast? . . . Adrenaline flowing, man? . . . Hot? Like you got too much blood in your body?

GRIFFIN. Yes.

LEE. And it makes you mad . . .

GRIFFIN. Yes.

LEE. (As Tyro.) *That's* how I feel, man—*all the time*.

GRIFFIN. (*Throwing and pinning Ty.*) Now it's your turn, Ty. Now *you* listen to me. I'm past the point of caring how you *feel*, man. You feel like shit? So do I. Your life doesn't mean anything to you? *Well, it means something to me! And I am NOT going to let you throw it away! Understand? UNDERSTAND!! NOW WHAT THE FUCK DO YOU NEED A GUN FOR?!?*

(Under tremendous pressure from GRIFFIN Tyro's fury breaks into what it really is—fear.)

LEE. (*Tyro—crying.*) *I get scared, man. I get scared. I get scared.*

GRIFFIN. (*Cradling Tyro.*) So do I, man. So do I. So do I. I won't let you down, Ty. I won't let you . . .

LEE. (*Standing, transforming to Lee.*) Mr. Griffin—did you get my portfolio?

GRIFFIN. Oh, shit . . .

LEE. (*Very grown up.*) Don't bother, Griff. I'll get it myself.

(LEE starts to exit.)

GRIFFIN. *GOD DAMN IT. SEÑORA!*

(STUDENTS appear as Señora.)

FREDDY. Tomas!
MARCO. Tomas!
CARLOS. Tomas!
LEE. (*Returning as Señora.*) Tomas!
GRIFFIN. *Señora!*
STUDENTS. Tomas!

GRIFFIN. WHY DIDN'T YOU DO A BETTER JOB WITH YOUR KIDS? WHY DO I HAVE TO CLEAN UP AFTER?

STUDENTS. (Señora) Tomas?

LEE. (Señora) Are you a Catholic, señor?

GRIFFIN. Yes . . . yes, I am.

LEE. (Señora) Do you believe in the Virgin Birth?

GRIFFIN. (*What?*) Do I beli . . . No, I don't think I do believe in the Virgin Birth.

STUDENTS. I do.

LEE. (Señora) In fact, it is the only kind of birth I *do* believe in.

MARCO. (Señora) Because the women in this neighborhood . . .

FREDDY. (Señora) . . . they are having babies . . .

STUDENTS. (Señora) . . . all—the—time . . .

LEE. (Señora) . . . and there are no fathers—anywhere. It is a fatherless world, señor.

GRIFFIN. Señora, I'm . . . I'm afraid I might not be much of an addition.

LEE. (Señora) Tomas, I would not worry too much about that. You remember when I said you were a bad man, an evil man?

GRIFFIN. It's OK, señora —I know you didn't mean it.

STUDENTS. No, I meant it.

LEE. (Señora) But, good or bad, I think you are what my son has needed . . .

STUDENTS. Tomas.

GRIFFIN. I hope so, Señora, I hope so. Because I'm scared, señora. I am scared.

(*JAMES enters above.*

LEE exits.
STUDENTS become STUDENTS again.)

JAMES. (*Amplified—as at an assembly.*) There's nothing to be scared about.

GRIFFIN. (*Backing offstage.*) I'm scared . . .

JAMES. The CTBS are far more an evaluation of the teachers than of the students.

GRIFFIN. I'm scared . . .

JAMES. So just do the best you can and make the school look good. You may begin.

(As JAMES speaks, HENRY appears playing basketball fiercely.)

STUDENTS. Way to go, Henry! Shoot that thing! Two points, Henry! . . .

(STUDENTS run off, leaving HENRY alone.)

ACT II

Scene 8

KENDALL appears—under a great deal of pressure. He has abandoned his proctoring of an exam to look for Henry.

KENDALL. Henry, you haven't finished the test.

HENRY (*Continuing to play ball beautifully.*) No, I haven't.

KENDALL. (*Starting back in.*) Come back inside.

HENRY (*Continuing to play.*) Sorry, Mr. K., I'm in the middle of a game with Ramon.

KENDALL. Ah, Mr. Cruz. How's life on the streets?

HENRY. Leave him alone. He's got a right to do what he likes.

KENDALL. Only up to a point. Most of what Ramon does, at least from what one hears, is felonious. Henry, *come back inside.*

HENRY. (*A challenge.*) Play a game, Mr. K.

KENDALL. No.

HENRY. Come on. Play me a game.

KENDALL. No, thank you.

HENRY. Hey, it's not hard.

KENDALL. Henry, time is passing.

HENRY. (*With an edge.*) Play a game. If you win . . . If you win, I'll finish the test.

KENDALL. (*After brief pause.*) The test is strictly timed.

(HENRY will now demonstrate the game elegantly as he describes its rules.)

HENRY. It's a simple game of "HORSE."

KENDALL. This isn't a game, Henry.

HENRY. Check it out! Whoever shoots and makes it, the other guy has to copy his shot. If he misses, he gets a letter. Whoever gets "HORSE" first loses.

KENDALL. Henry . . .

HENRY. You're lucky I'm in a good mood today. I'll even give you a break and take H-O-R. Come on, it's not hard.

(HENRY tosses the ball to KENDALL who looks foolish with it in his hands.)

KENDALL. *(Dropping the ball.)* I'll count to three.
HENRY. *(Retrieving the ball.)* You won't even *try*?
KENDALL. *(Final ultimatum.)* One.
HENRY. OK. H-O-R-S.
KENDALL. Two.
HENRY. *Come on. You only have to sink one.*
KENDALL. *Three!*
HENRY. *(Throwing the ball at Kendall hard.) Take the ball and shoot!*
KENDALL. *(Exploding.) I'm not here to make a fool of myself!*
HENRY. *(Matching him.) Me neither!*
KENDALL. Henry, nobody's trying to make a fool . . .
HENRY. *THEN WHY THE FUCK ARE YOU GIVING ME A TEST YOU KNOW I CAN'T PASS!*
KENDALL. *(After brief pause.)* You have to take tests, Hank.
HENRY. They give you one word and say pick one of the following five words that means the same as the first word . . . and I don't even know the first word. Times fifty questions. Times all day for five days. You want to know how I feel? Play me some b-ball, Mr. Kendall, and I'll *show* you how I feel.

(KENDALL stands helpless.)

HENRY. Come on, Ramon. Let's get out of here.
KENDALL. *(Quietly.)* I'll get you through the test.

HENRY. (*Turning.*) You will?

(*JAMES enters in the background.*)

KENDALL. Yes.
HENRY. (*Delighted.*) How?
KENDALL. (*To James as he arrives center.*) I told him he could cheat.

(*Overjoyed, HENRY runs off.*)

JAMES. Let me see if I've got this right. . .
KENDALL. *I told him he could cheat!*
LARKIN. (*Appearing above.*) OK, gentlemen, pencils down.
JAMES. (*Unbelieving.*) And what grade would you like him to get? 90? 100?
KENDALL. He doesn't even have to pass. Just something that isn't humiliating.
JAMES. (*After some consideration.*) Very well. Bring Henry in and we'll start writing the answers on his sneakers.

(*KENDALL is dumfounded.*)

JAMES. That's how it's done, isn't it? I assume you would know.
KENDALL. What have you done with the real Mitchell James?
JAMES. You didn't visit me in the hospital after the robbery . . .
KENDALL. I was very busy . . .

JAMES. Well—Henry did.

(Loud metallic CLANK.)

ACT II

Scene 9

LARKIN. Next is the true-and-false section. Most people say this is a piece of cake, but for me discovering the difference between the two has been my life's work. You have seven minutes to work it out.

(Metallic CRASH.)

LARKIN. You may begin.

(The rooftop: GRIFFIN hyped for good news; LEE, withdrawn, looks at the closed portfolio which lies on the floor in front of him.)

GRIFFIN. How did the interview go, Lee?
LEE. Bad.
GRIFFIN. Why? Were you scared?
LEE. Yeah, that must be it—I was scared.
GRIFFIN. You had nothing to be frightened of. There can't be too many kids who have a portfolio like yours.
LEE. No, I'm sure of that.
GRIFFIN. Did Tyro get it to school on time?
LEE. Yes.

GRIFFIN. (*Delighted*.) See—I told you he could change.

LEE. Yeah, you told me.

GRIFFIN. Can I see it?

(*LEE throws the portfolio open. It has been hideously vandalized.*)

GRIFFIN. Oh, shit.

LEE. No. At least not all of it. Some of it's blood. Some of it's food. Some of it's puke.

GRIFFIN. (*Backing away*.) Oh, Lee . . .

LEE. YOU WANTED TO LOOK AT IT—WELL, LOOK AT IT! No! Don't look at what's on the paper. That's a picture of a bottle and a stupid orange—it makes me laugh—LOOK AT THE EDGE! See, it isn't ripped. It's CUT! With a very sharp knife! I've got a picture of my brother in there somewhere, but that cut, that cut is the best picture of my brother anybody could ever do. Or look at this one with the crayons all over it. That's the kids. Or this one, I don't even know what's on it—could be the kids, but it's probably my mother cause you know she's always sick and you have to use something to clean up after. You know what this is really? . . . It is a TREMENDOUS, FANTASTIC picture of my family. But you know what? . . . They didn't understand that up at Art and Design.

GRIFFIN. I'm sorry, Lee.

LEE. *Don't say you're sorry Griff.* You're *not* sorry. You got what *you* wanted . . . I'm ready to go to that home now. Why not? I don't have a family anymore. (*LEE runs off*.)

GRIFFIN. That's not what I wanted, Lee. Lee! Not like this. Lee! Not like . . .

(Loud metallic CRASH!
Lee's family's apartment.
The STUDENTS stripped to the waist, dressed in sweat pants, appear as Tyro. Speeches overlap. A PRISON RIOT of sound.)

FREDDY. (Tyro) Sorry, man, I didn't mean . . .

CARLOS (Tyro) You were asking too much, man . . .

MARCO (Tyro) I did the best I could . . .

STUDENTS. (Tyro) I LOST THE JOB!

GRIFFIN. *(Over the top.) HOW COULD YOU DO THIS?!?*

MARCO (Tyro) I warned you, man . . .

CARLOS (Tyro) You were pushing me too hard, man .
. .

FREDDY (Tyro) All you care about is Lee, man . . .

STUDENTS. (Tyro) ALL YOU CARE ABOUT IS LEE!

GRIFFIN. FORGET LEE! HOW COULD YOU DO THIS TO *YOURSELF*?

FREDDY (Tyro) You don't care about me, man . . .

MARCO (Tyro) You don't give a shit . . .

CARLOS (Tyro) Man, all you care about is yourself . .
.

STUDENTS. (Tyro) ALL YOU CARE ABOUT IS YOURSELF!

GRIFFIN. OK—*ME*, THEN? HOW COULD YOU DO THIS TO *ME?* I AM THE ONE HUMAN BEING ON THIS *PLANET* THAT DOESN'T WANT YOU *DEAD*!

STUDENTS. (Tyro) FUCK YOU, WHITE BOY!

GRIFFIN. (*With profound sorrow.*) . . . and you're going to die, Tyro . . . I'll miss you, Ty, 'cause it made me feel less alone in the world knowing that somebody besides me knew that every day was life and death. It just never *occurred* to me that anybody who knew that *would be STUPID enough to pick DEATH.* (*GRIFFIN strips to start a costume change into sweats.*)

CARLOS (*Tyro—pleading.*) No, man, I don't want to die . . .

FREDDY (Tyro) Man, that's not what I want . . .

MARCO (Tyro) Don't be saying that . . .

GRIFFIN. (*Covering his ears with his hands.*) Pardon me, Ty. I can't hear you.

STUDENTS. (*Tyro—fiercely honest.*) *I DON'T WANT TO DIE!*

GRIFFIN. (*Shouting —hands over ears.*) I'm sorry, Ty. *I can't hear you.* Well, you know how it is. You Hispanics refuse to learn English. Secure borders. Welfare state, Ty.

STUDENTS. NO, MAN. I DON'T WANT TO DIE!!!

GRIFFIN. I CAN'T HEAR YOU!

(*Removes hands from his ears as TYRO disappears.*)

GRIFFIN. (*A final benediction on Ty:*) Die quickly, Ty, so the rest of us can rest in peace.

(*Loud WHISTLES.*
STUDENTS and GRIFFIN put on sweat shirts for the event of the year:)

ACT II

Scene 10

WHISTLES are blown.
HENRY runs on wearing Trinity Mission School sweats
and announces:

HENRY. (*Flying.*) Laaaaadies and Geeeeeeeentlemen!
Welcome to the contest of the year where Age faces Youth:
The Student-Faculty End-of-Term Tackle Basketball
Tournament!

(*STUDENTS and FACULTY, all in sweats, enter*
cheering.
KENDALL enters a moment after suited up for the game.
He looks ridiculous—sweat shirt tucked neatly into
sweat pants.)

KENDALL. (*To the faculty huddle.*) *Nobody—for any*
reason—is to throw the ball to me. Is that agreed?
FACULTY Ohhhhhhh, No!
STUDENTS. (*Coming out of their huddle.*) Kick some
ass!

(*The game begins.*)

HENRY. The ball is up. Tap to the students! All right!
Go, students!

*(All PLAYERS run off stage left. KENDALL follows
them at his own dignified trot.*
*HENRY—flying on a wonderful playful energy—
announces the action that we cannot see,
unselfconsciously mirroring the plays of the game in
his body.)*

HENRY. Ruiz shoots. Cruz rebounds. Cruz passes to
Ruiz, Ruiz shoots. Misses. Rebound—Fr. Larkin! Larkin
to Griffin who takes it up court.

*(The PLAYERS thunder across the stage, exiting stage
right where the action continues out of audience sight.*
*Then KENDALL enters and leisurely walks across stage
with great dignity.)*

HENRY. And Mr. Kendall comes up court on the
slowest fast break in the history of basketball! Way to go,
Mr. K.!

*(KENDALL acknowledges the roar of the crowd and
continues offstage unperturbed.*
*Once KENDALL is offstage, HENRY resumes his play-
by-play.)*

HENRY. Larkin shoots, misses, he's getting old. James
rebounds. James to Griffin who drives up the key, fakes,
pivots, passes to Larkin at the top of the key, he shoots,
he SCORES! Faculty takes the first lead of the game. GO,
STUDENTS.

(The PLAYERS run across the stage and off stage left.

*KENDALL again walks leisurely across the court,
unbothered by the fact that the game is passing him by
entirely.)*

HENRY. Cruz takes the ball up court. He's driving it.
Cruz shoots. He scores! TWO POINTS! Way to go,
Cruzer! Tie Ball!

*(This time KENDALL hasn't even made it off stage as the
HERD thunders past him. HE reverses direction and
starts back towards the faculty basket. As all the others
rush off stage, KENDALL stops center to tie his
sneaker.)*

HENRY. James brings the ball up court, passes to
Larkin, who turns and passes to . . . KENDALL!

*(The ball rolls on stage to Kendall's feet. KENDALL looks
at the unfamiliar object and throws it back off stage
where he feels it belongs.)*

HENRY. Kendall passes back to Larkin who takes the
ball up court, he passes to James who passes off to . . .

(The ball flies back on stage.)

HENRY. KENDALL!

*(KENDALL catches the ball, looks at it, looks offstage
with annoyance at the faculty members who are trying
to force him into the game. HE passes the ball
offstage.)*

HENRY. Kendall passes to James who passes to Griffin who passes to . . .

(Again the ball flies into KENDALL's hands.)

HENRY. KENDALL!

(KENDALL contemplates the ball seriously as the CROWD begins to CHANT for him to join the game.)

ALL. *(With HENRY leading the chant.)* KENDALL! KENDALL! KENDALL!

(KENDALL rises to the challenge. Very calmly, without the hint of a rush, KENDALL takes the ball up court and offstage to wild CHEERING.)

HENRY. Way to go, Mr. K!!! Kendall takes the ball to the top of the key. He stops. He shoots!
ALL. AIR BALL!
HENRY. Rebound—James. James to Griffin to Larkin to KENDALL to Larkin to KENDALL to Griffin to KENDALL. KENDALL stops. He puts it back up.

(ALL inhale.)

HENRY. HE *SCORES*! TWO POINTS!

(ALL cheer. KENDALL, shy and extremely pleased, comes to center acknowledging the crowd response. TEACHERS and STUDENTS pat him on the back.)

HENRY. (*Taking a camera out of his pocket.*) Hey, Burke! Over here!

(*ALL assemble around KENDALL for a picture to memorialize the event.*)

HENRY. OK. One—two—*THREE!*

(*FLASH! as HENRY takes the picture. Then, in an instant of silence:*)

JAMES. Henry, let me see that camera.

(*ALL start to run off. HENRY, not having heard James, calls to the group for one more picture.*)

HENRY. OK, one more!

(*CHEERING, the GROUP forms around KENDALL again. FLASH! as HENRY takes another photo.*)

JAMES. (*More forcefully.*) Henry, let me see that camera.

(*Cheering, the GROUP exits.*)

JAMES. *Let me see the camera.*
HENRY. (*Backing away.*) It's mine.
LARKIN. (*Re-entering.*) What's up?
JAMES. Henry won't let me see his camera.
HENRY. *It's mine.*

JAMES. I didn't say it wasn't.

(The other TEACHERS and STUDENTS drift in.)

GRIFFIN. *(Breathless.)* Come on, guys, I can't play them myself.

LARKIN. *(Anticipating trouble.)* Look, there are a lot of cameras like this one . . .

JAMES. Mine has my initials on it.

(A beat of silence as HENRY checks the camera for initials. LARKIN realizes what's up.)

LARKIN. Let's settle this later, Mitch . . .

(LARKIN tries to lead the group back into the game.)

JAMES. *(Holding his ground.)* Henry has a camera that was stolen from my apartment. We will settle it *right now* or I will call the police and have them settle it.

LARKIN. *(After a tense moment.)* Freddy, set up an inter-squad scrimmage.

(STUDENTS exit.
A moment of tense silence:)

LARKIN. *(Trying for a reasonable tone.)* There are a great many ways in which Henry could have come by this camera . . .

JAMES. *He stole it.*

LARKIN. *(With the camera, seeing the initials.)* . . . but what can't be denied is that he is in possession of stolen goods . . . (*LARKIN has been betrayed and knows it, but still tries to get Henry off lightly:*) . . . and the penalty for that according to the school rules is suspension, so, Henry, you're suspended for a week—(*LARKIN again tries to lead them all back to the game.*)

JAMES. (*Unyielding.*) SUSPENDED! SUSPENDED? You suspend a kid for fighting in the hall. A student broke into my apartment, robbed from me and beat me seriously enough to put me in the hospital.

HENRY. I didn't do that.

JAMES. Then how did you get this camera?

HENRY. Fr. Larkin knows what I did and didn't do.

JAMES. (*After brief pause.*) You *knew?*

LARKIN. (*After brief pause.*) Henry, would you step out for a second, please?

HENRY. Can I say something first?

LARKIN. Yes.

HENRY. (*Costly and true.*) I don't want to get thrown out of this school. (*HENRY exits.*)

GRIFFIN. Look, graduation is just a couple of weeks . . .

JAMES. *Shit!*

KENDALL. (*After brief pause.*) May I?

LARKIN. Burke . . .

KENDALL. Mitch, you have been wronged, seriously wronged.

JAMES. Yes, I have, Burke, and I will not be mocked.

KENDALL. I have no intention of mocking you . . . How's your camera, Mitch? Not that it's about the camera, but how is it? Still in working order?

JAMES. Jesus . . .

KENDALL. How're you feeling these days, Mitch? It looked to me like you were playing some pretty good ball out there, not that I'm a connoisseur . . . but, Mitch, how's your health?

(JAMES does not answer.)

KENDALL. What did Henry get on your last test, Mitch? Not that it will qualify him for an early admission to Harvard, but was it higher than it was at the start of the year?

JAMES. I am not a punching bag. I am a professional teacher.

KENDALL. *(Closer and closer to the heart.)* Exactly. And one of the things we profess is to take some of the evil these kids throw at us and hand them back something better. Mitch, I would take it as a personal favor if you would do that on this occasion.

(No response.)

KENDALL. It's a judgement call—I know that, I respect that—but Mitch? If you get him thrown out of this school? I never want to hear another *word* out of you about how to teach anybody anything.

JAMES. So I'm the villain?

KENDALL. Or the hero.

JAMES. *(After a pause, to Larkin.)* If he is not thrown out of this school immediately, I will take legal action against him. And the school. *(JAMES exits.)*

LARKIN. *(To Kendall.)* Call Henry in.

(KENDALL goes for Henry.)

GRIFFIN. *(Softly.)* Ed, now's the time to buy the whore the cup of coffee.

(KENDALL returns with HENRY. HENRY, knowing he's in Larkin's hands now, is sure he is safe.)

LARKIN. *(At great cost.)* Henry, pack your locker.
HENRY. *(After a pause.)* I don't care. *(HENRY exits.)*
GRIFFIN. Walk him to his apartment, Burke. Walk him past the hookers and the dealers. Sit down at the kitchen table, open a book and start teaching him there.
KENDALL. I'll be in my classroom, Ed. *(KENDALL exits sadly.)*
GRIFFIN. *(Shouting after Kendall.) It has nothing to do with classrooms. It's a blood covenant.*
LARKIN. *(After brief pause.)* I'm too old for this.
GRIFFIN. Was it any easier when you were younger?
LARKIN. You tell me . . . No screaming accusations?
GRIFFIN. I just did the same thing to Tyro. I wrote him off. It's real ugly, isn't it? You just can't do it. It's the one thing that would make life bearable and you just can't do it.
LARKIN. *(Slamming a locker.)* Shit.
GRIFFIN. Shit.
LARKIN. *(Locker.)* SHIT!

(HENRY, with backpack, walks across the stage, stopping to look at Larkin and Griffin. HE then walks out the front door of the school forever.)

LARKIN. I want to go to confession.

GRIFFIN. Go find a priest.

LARKIN. I don't need a priest. I am a priest. I need somebody who's gone far enough that he might understand. (*Kneeling in the center of the basketball court:*) Bless me, Tom, for I have sinned. It's been what—twenty years?—since my last confession. I want to be forgiven for doing all that I've done to keep this school open hoping that it would do some good. I want to be forgiven for the distance between what I am and what they need.

GRIFFIN. (*Laying on hands.*) I forgive you your sins in the name of Henry and Tyro and all the others.

LARKIN. Thanks.

GRIFFIN. (*Exhausted, exiting.*) I have to go see Tyro.

LARKIN. (*Sitting on the floor, exhausted.*) Let him die, Tom. Don't stand in his way. It's what he wants.

GRIFFIN. (*Equally exhausted.*) God, I envy you. I wish I could give up.

LARKIN. Or dump him someplace. Get him out of the way so Lee can have a clear shot.

GRIFFIN. Wait. You're not forgiven yet. For your penance you have to get me a high school diploma.

LARKIN. For Henry?

GRIFFIN. Tyro. See, Tyro wants to join the army and make something of his life, but he can't without a . . .

LARKIN. He told you that?

GRIFFIN. (*Going to Larkin.*) No, how could he—he doesn't even know yet. Ed, get me a diploma.

LARKIN. (*Rising.*) I can't do that.

GRIFFIN. I trust you to do the right thing . . . *for the good of the boy.*

(LARKIN exits.
GRIFFIN starts quietly to cry as he makes his way back to
*   the apartment.)*

GRIFFIN. . . . and I forgive me my sins in the name of
. . . Oh, fuck . . . I am so, so sorry . . . I'm sorry, Ty . . .
I know the army isn't the life you wanted, Ty, but you're
going to be in great physical shape and you're going to
be—all that you can be, Ty . . . I know it's not the life
you want, but, hell, Ty, I don't get the life I want either . .
. I've got to get out of here . . . Somebody, please, MAKE
ME—A LAWYER!

(KENDALL and JAMES appear, dressed in suits and ties.
*   They will strip and redress GRIFFIN in a business suit*
*   while he speaks:)*

KENDALL and JAMES. (*Singing a doo-wop.*) Shoo
wop. Shoo bop. It's graduation . . . (*KENDALL and*
JAMES continue shoo-wopping under:)
GRIFFIN. (*Laughing/crying.*) So Lee's mother wouldn't
do anything about the notice to evict and—with Ty and Lee
gone—sure as hell she'd end up in the streets so I thought,
Shit, I've got to get this lady some housing. So I found her
this home for battered women, but when we get there, they
say to me there's no room in the inn, and I say, Wait a
minute, you told me . . . No, that was two weeks ago,
they say. I say, So what? She's here now. And they say
they couldn't hold a place for her. There are other homeless
people, you know. So I say—So what? Throw them out.
They've been homeless before. They're used to it.

LARKIN. (*Dressed in formal clerics.*)
Counterproductive.

GRIFFIN. (*Through fierce, bitter laughter.*) And it gets
crazier and crazier every place we go. The last place we
went, they told me she was beaten by *the wrong person*. I
said what the fuck do you mean? I know.
Counterproductive. And they say, we only accept women
who've been beaten by their husbands. We don't believe it's
serious if she's beaten by a son. And I say, What are you
talking about? Her husbands are old and slow; the kid is in
his prime and full of drugs and they say, Sorry, we have
our rules and I say, No, wait, I'm her husband. I beat her
all the time. I'll beat her here and now if you'll give her a
room.

(*STUDENTS, dressed beautifully for graduation, appear.
KENDALL and JAMES stop their singing and go
upstage to arrange last minute details of the graduation.*)

LARKIN. Is señora coming to graduation?

GRIFFIN. (*Near emotional collapse*) I don't know. That
shelter, man. It's a human garbage dump. And it's *BIG!* I
took one look at it and I thought, Jesus, there ought to be
a government program—and then I realized—this *is* The
Government Program. It's our version of the final solution.
You were right from the start, Ed. It's the police, the
federal government, Japan, us—we *want* it this way. But it
isn't ecology, Ed. Nature never had anything to do with it.

LARKIN. (*Reaching for Griffin.*) Look, you did what
you had to do for Lee . . .

GRIFFIN. (*Fierce.*) *Ed. I threw Lee's mother in a garbage dump so I could get my ass out of here in one piece.*

LARKIN. OK, so you didn't empty hell. So you're no medieval saint. But believe me—one baby gets out . . .

(LEE enters center dressed for graduation white suit, white hat—stunning)

LARKIN. . . . it makes everything else worthwhile.

GRIFFIN. (*Still in his own world.*) Ed, that's *such* a lie . . .

LARKIN. (*As GRIFFIN sees Lee.*) Really, Tom? (*To Lee.*) That's quite a hat.

LEE. You like it?

LARKIN. You look like a pimp.

LEE. Thank you.

(LARKIN moves away some distance, leaving GRIFFIN and LEE some privacy before the ceremony.)

ACT II

Scene 11

Silence.

GRIFFIN. You made it . . . Congratulations, Lee.

LEE. I couldn't have made it without you.

GRIFFIN. (*Touched.*) Thanks—I was hoping to hear something like that tonight.

LEE. (*An edge.*) I mean, I never would of graduated if you hadn't thrown my brother in the army and my mother in a shelter . . . Thanks a lot, Griff.

(SLAM!)

GRIFFIN. (*Hurt.*) I feel bad about that, Lee.

LEE. (*Forgiving.*) That's okay . . .

GRIFFIN. (*Cold.*) . . . but you know, I didn't see a lot of you when I was trying to get them placed. How is life on Staten Island, Lee?

(SLAM!)

GRIFFIN. See a lot of videos out there, do you?

(LARKIN begins to overhear the conversation.)

LEE. (*Honest.*) I wanted to be there . . .

GRIFFIN. (*Understanding.*) Oh . . .

LEE. . . . but the psychiatrist at the home said it wasn't good for me to help.

GRIFFIN. (*An accusation.*) The *psychiatrist* said?

LEE. You wanted me in a home, didn't you? That's part of it. Rugs on the floors and all.

LARKIN. (*Trying to save the night.*) Tom, could I . . .

GRIFFIN. (*Hand up—"Stay out of it?"*) You remember Pedro? I worked real hard all year long to get him to speak English. Now that he can, I don't much like what he says.

LEE. Mr. Griffin, I don't like not having a family.

GRIFFIN. Yeah, well . . . work it out with your shrink.

LEE. (*Please.*) You'll be back to visit?

GRIFFIN. (*Honestly.*) They say first year law school is pretty rough.

LEE. (*Edged.*) Yeah? Compared to what?

KENDALL. (*Calling the group together.*) Graduates.

(*LEE starts to walk away.*)

GRIFFIN. (*Sorrow and anger and more sorrow.*) Look, *I'm sorry.* I did what I could. I tried to move the world and it fell on me . . .

LEE. On *you?* . . .

GRIFFIN. . . . on us. Look, let's not fight about the pain. There's plenty of that to go around. (*From a full heart:*) I—am—*proud* of you. You're worth the world. And you made it, Lee.

LEE. I made it . . . even with your help.

GRIFFIN. (*Lightening.*) Yeah, even with my help. *Congratulations.*(*Silence.*) I don't have anything to give you . . .

LEE. (*Simple truth.*) I'm graduating, Griff. You gave me that. (*Putting out a hand.*) Goodbye, Mr. Griffin.

GRIFFIN. Goodbye, Lee.

(*LEE and GRIFFIN shake hands, then move awkwardly into a tight embrace.*
STUDENTS and FACULTY form graduation around them.)

KENDALL. Ladies and gentlemen, the national anthem.

ALL. (*Singing out beautifully.*) Oooooooo say can you see! And the home of the brave!

JAMES. Our valedictorian, Marco Ruiz.

MARCO. (*Taking center.*) Tonight we graduate and that is very hopeful. Our parents left their homes and came to this country in the hope of finding something better and giving it to their children. By mistake, they came to New York. So now it is our duty to succeed at school and give something better to them. But it is foolish for me to keep speaking to you, our parents, since you do not understand the language I speak as I only half understand yours. Thank you.

LARKIN. Thank you for that moving and beautiful speech. And now, ladies and gentlemen, the awarding of the diplomas. Please come forward as your name is called. Name . . . Name . . . Name . . . Name . . .

(As LARKIN calls "names," ALL move back, applauding and cheering for the graduates, leaving LEE center in a brilliant white spot.)

LARKIN. *Lidelfo Cortez*!

GRIFFIN. (*Whistling and screaming above the group.*) Yeah, LEE!

(All APPLAUSE suddenly becomes the menacing sound of Tyro's applause. Tyro, high, has arrived in the middle of the ceremony.

HENRY re-enters to join the STUDENTS in portraying Tyro.

Eventually, the full company (except LARKIN) will do Tyro, but on the sections where Tyro is dealing with his most serious pain . . . that's a territory that only GRIFFIN and LEE can enter.)

STUDENTS. (*Tyro—taking over the ceremony.*) Hey, you look handsome, Lee.
LEE. Tyro?
STUDENTS (*Tyro*) *I like the hat.*
GRIFFIN. One kid gets out makes it all worthwhile, huh, Ed?
LARKIN. Shit! Tyro.
LEE. What are you doing here, Ty?
MARCO (*Señora*) You know, that's the funny thing about my family . . .
GRIFFIN. Señora . . .
FREDDY (*Señora*) Lee's the better boy but he's never there.
MARCO (*Señora*) . . . but you just look over your shoulder and there's Tyro. . .
STUDENTS (*Señora*) Just like a shadow.

(SLAM!)

LARKIN. I warned you, Tom. I don't want him in here!
GRIFFIN. You got permission to be here tonight, Ty?
STUDENTS (*Tyro*) *I don't need permission, man.*
GRIFFIN. 'Cause the army isn't like school, Ty. You can't graduate yourself from the army, boy. They're real anal about things like that.

(SLAM!)

LARKIN. (*Trying to save the night.*) Mr. Kendall . . .

KENDALL. Now let us sing our closing hymn . . .
ALL. (*Singing out.*) Holy God, we praise thy name . .
.

STUDENTS, KENDALL and JAMES. (Tyro) *I mean
it's nice the way you overcame your environment and all to
get your diploma . . .*
LARKIN. *Ty, sit down and be quiet.*
STUDENTS, KENDALL and JAMES. (Tyro) *You're a
real success.*

(SLAM!)

LARKIN. Tom, call the police.
LEE. The police? NO!
LARKIN. Tom!
LEE. NO! DON'T GET HIM IN ANY TROUBLE!
LARKIN. CALL THE POLICE!

(SLAM!)

LEE. (*Exploding as Tyro.*) *Man, that's all you know
how to do—throw me out of here! Is that like your career
goal, man?*
GRIFFIN. (*After brief silence.*) What do you want, Ty?
LEE, STUDENTS, KENDALL and JAMES. (Tyro) *I
WANT TO GIVE A SPEECH!*

LEE. (*Tyro—after brief silence.*) A graduation speech . .
. and then I'll go.
GRIFFIN. Let him give a speech . . .
LARKIN. I want him out of here.

GRIFFIN. We're always throwing him out. Let him give a . . .

(SLAM!)

GRIFFIN, LEE, STUDENTS, KENDALL and JAMES. (Tyro) WELCOME TO TRINITY MISSION SCHOOL!

LEE. (Tyro) You all made it back except the few who chose the streets . . .

GRIFFIN. (Tyro) Look out the windows . . .

GRIFFIN, LEE, STUDENTS, KENDALL and JAMES. (Tyro) YOU'RE DIFFERENT FROM THEM!

LEE. (*Tyro on fire.*) Do I have it right, Father?

GRIFFIN. (Tyro) You think I didn't learn anything here . . .

GRIFFIN, LEE, STUDENTS, KENDALL and JAMES (Tyro) I LEARNED A LOT!

GRIFFIN and LEE. (Tyro) . . . but, you see, your speech doesn't help me much because where it *ended*—that's where I need it to *begin!*

GRIFFIN, LEE, STUDENTS, KENDALL and JAMES. (Tyro) WHAT DO I DO NOW, FR. LARKIN?

(SLAM!)

LARKIN. Fine, Ty. You're finally going to get what you want. (*LARKIN starts to exit to call the police.*)

STUDENTS. HUH!

(LARKIN, GRIFFIN and LEE freeze.)

GRIFFIN. Oh, good. A gun! Why didn't I think of that?

STUDENTS, KENDALL and JAMES. (Tyro) NO, MAN. THIS ISN'T A GUN. THIS IS A HEARING AID. IT HELPS PEOPLE LIKE YOU HEAR!

LEE. I hear you, Ty . . .

GRIFFIN. I hear you . . .

(SLAM! GRIFFIN and LEE—as Tyro—howl in pain.)

LEE. (Tyro) *I don't have a place to live . . .*

GRIFFIN. (Tyro) I *don't have a family . . .*

LEE. (Tyro) *I don't have a diploma . . .*

GRIFFIN. (Tyro) *I don't have a job . . .*

LEE. (Tyro) I DON'T HAVE A LIFE.

GRIFFIN and LEE. (Tyro) I'VE GOT NOTHING, MAN. I'VE GOT *NOTHING!*

(First GUN SHOT.
ALL but LEE, GRIFFIN and LARKIN run for cover.)

LARKIN. Oh, shit. Burke, call the . . .

GRIFFIN. You do that, Burke . . .

LEE, STUDENTS, KENDALL and JAMES. SAGA WAS BIG . . .

GRIFFIN. Fights in this neighborhood last twenty or thirty seconds . . .

LEE, STUDENTS, KENDALL and JAMES. SAGA WAS BUILT!

GRIFFIN. We ought to be done by the time you get back!

LEE, STUDENTS, KENDALL and JAMES. SAGA HAS TO ANSWER FOR THE BLOOD!

GRIFFIN. You're gonna be all right, Ty . . .

STUDENTS, KENDALL and JAMES. (Tyro) I'VE GOT NOTHING!

LEE. We can make it work!!!

GRIFFIN. TY!

STUDENTS, KENDALL and JAMES (Tyro) WHAT ABOUT ME, MAN?

LEE. TY!

STUDENTS, KENDALL and JAMES (Tyro.) WHAT ABOUT ME?

(GRIFFIN and LEE rush Tyro.
GUN SHOT.
GRIFFIN and LEE embrace—holding each other up. We are uncertain as to who was shot. The rest of the CAST moves upstage saying as they go. . .)

JAMES. You're trying to change something that isn't supposed to change . . .

KENDALL. *(Overlapping.)* Someone has to be the bottom ten percent on standardized tests . . .

HENRY. *(Overlapping.)* So what am I gonna be, man, a lawyer? . . .

MARCO. *(Overlapping.)* So it is our duty to succeed at school and give something better to them . . .

HENRY. *(Overlapping.)* So what are they, evolutionary mistakes? . . .

(GRIFFIN and LEE step apart. BOTH are covered in blood. LEE falls to the ground.)

ACT II

Scene 12

(A funeral—as at opening. A STUDENT appears with holy water. GRIFFIN holds LEE and rocks him.)

LARKIN. *(Enraged—putting on a stole.) Now* who do we bury? Well, we bury Lee in the ground.
GRIFFIN. *(Howling.)* NO!
LARKIN. *(Sprinkling water.)* Hell, that's normal. That won't even make the papers.
GRIFFIN. Noooooooo!

(JAMES pulls GRIFFIN away from the boy. KENDALL takes care of LEE on the ground. LARKIN circles the stage sprinkling holy water.)

LARKIN. We bury . . . we bury Henry in the streets . . . We bury Tyro in a jail . . .
GRIFFIN. *(Straining against JAMES towards Lee.)* Nooooooooooo!
LARKIN. We bury Señora in a shelter . . .
GRIFFIN. Noooooooooo!
LARKIN. . . . and things *are* the way they're *supposed* to be.

(STUDENT, KENDALL and JAMES disappear.
LEE slowly rises from where he had fallen.
Around the place where he had fallen is a chalk outline of his body.

GRIFFIN, LARKIN and LEE contemplate it.)

LARKIN. *(A final desperate blessing.)* May the angels lead us all into paradise.

(The sound of CHILDREN playing in a playground grows and grows.
LEE, GRIFFIN and LARKIN slowly back off stage.
SPOTLIGHT on the bloody outline of the body.
Loud, sustained school BELL.)

BLACKOUT

Author's Notes:

True story.

There was to be a memorial mass at "Trinity Mission School" on the occasion of the death of a teacher's mother. Before the mass began, Father Principal asked the students if there were any of their own relatives that they would like to have remembered at the mass. Slowly, the kids started to talk about the dead of their families and told a bit of their stories. They spoke of grandfathers, uncles, older brothers, grandmothers, older brothers, aunts, older brothers, friends, older brothers . . . brothers . . . brothers . . . brothers. . . We never got to the mass that day because time ran out before the list of dead older brothers did.

End of story.

We live in a country—the most prosperous in the history of the world—where one of the leading causes of death of non-white young men is violence. This is a tragedy so vast that it feels, as Tom Griffin says, like "our version of the Final Solution." *Stand-Up Tragedy* tries to move from the numbing size of that social issue to the feeling heart of the problem: the beyond-limits value of the life of one person . . . one person that our way of life has marked for an early death.

Facing this death within the confines of a "school" play is not easy since "school" plays are generally Cinderella stories and people get *very* upset when you shoot Cinderella. The story, according to our prevailing myth, *should* go: Teacher (white) reaches out to talented Student-in-need (non-white) and transforms Student's life before midnight strikes (graduation). It's a lovely story and should be celebrated whenever it happens, but there's *another* story that we have to face if we're ever to stop adding names to that dead-older-brother list. That story was best summed up by a brilliant young teacher at Trinity, Steve Macuk, who used to say, "The kids are dying and it's not even making the papers."

I have tried to write the story of what I saw and heard while teaching in the way that I saw it—packed and pulsing with life. Not well-made and neatly organized, but chaotic, muscular, frequently very funny, relentless, with moments of deep understanding emerging when the sheer volume of city-sound explodes into silence.

I have tried to write a play in which every character is a hero. Audience members have occasionally asked why a certain character (it can be almost any one of them) is so cynical. And my answer is that there are *no* cynics in this play. These teachers and students see impossible odds stacked against them and they tell the truth about it. (Even Fr. Larkin's version of the Christmas story, which may *sound* cynical with its nightmares and bloodshed, is far truer to the gospel than our usual Hallmark version.) In spite of the terrible truths that confront them, these teachers and students turn up daily and try to pass on a better world at 3:00 than they found at 8:00 that morning. They're not cynics. They're heroes—every one of them.

(The same is true of Señora and Tyro who are, clearly, facing the toughest odds of all.)

The play is *packed* with words and they are meant to go fast—not just to buzz through the text, but because speed was an essential component of the neighborhood. The press of events was frequently overwhelming and the pace inside the school matched the streets. Periods at the school were twenty-five minutes long rather than the usual forty or forty-five. The principal's reason for this was simple: "The first and last ten minutes of most classes are small talk. These kids don't have *time* for small talk. *Teach the middle twenty-five minutes and get on with it!*" And we did. The bell would ring and off we'd go.

(That was as true of Ron Link's original production as it was of the school. Each act ran approximately 1:10.)

The language of the play is very rough. The theaters where we worked were always on guard in previews for objections to "language," but there were surprisingly few complaints. (I think in some bizarre way the fact that some of the roughest language comes from a priest makes it acceptable. I don't know why this should be.) I have been asked if I have any objections to subsequent productions softening the language. The answer is, *"Yes, Goddamn it!"* But—what the hell—change it if you feel you're working in a community where nobody's heard these words before. My goal in writing the play was not to set any records for use of Anglo-Saxon expletives, but to tell the story of the kids and their teachers.

One thing must *not* be changed. The set must be minimal with very few props. *Stand-Up Tragedy* is a play about transformations that happen within people and they happen at the speed of thought. Ron Link understood this instinctively and much rehearsal time was spent on creating those instantaneous transformations. The students (in the text, all Hispanic; in production, more diverse) were absolutely vital in inventing and creating the constantly changing worlds of the play.

I wish any production of *Stand-Up Tragedy* the luck I had with the original production: a theater as wonderful as the Mark Taper Forum, a director as resourceful as Ron

Link, and designers, cast and crew whose contributions to the final work were absolutely massive.

Finally, a closing last word from Griffin: "Let's fuck up that old ecology of evil. What else is life for?"

COSTUME PLOT

GENERAL WARDROBE INFO:

There are doubles and some triples of almost everything. The doubles are on daily wash as well as the over tops that the students wear and student jeans except Ray Oriel.

Students receive entirely clean clothes between matinee and evening shows, including knee pads. You will find that the students are soaked after every performance.

BLOOD

WHITE RAYON SUIT

I have been spraying a light coat of Scotch Guard on the front of the jacket and a little on the back.

At the end of the show it seems to be very helpful to the dry cleaner to wipe off as much blood as possible. The pants and tie don't need to be wiped off as there is not as much on them. I have been washing the shirt, it seems to do fine.

Blood will be on different articles of clothing every night. For the most part it wipes of off all except the rayon suit.

Jack Coleman's tie is even hand-washable, the shirt should be rinsed out at the end of the show before being put in the washer. We have had a wet warm towel for him at curtain call when he changes out of the shirt and tie into the blue sweatshirt on stage left.

TOM GRIFFIN
PRESETS
<u>ON</u> <u>STAGE</u>
  Brown tweed sport coat
  Brown herringbone overcoat
  Trinity sweatshirt (Act II)

<u>STAGE</u> <u>RIGHT</u>
  Blue checked dress shirt
  Taupe print tie (Set at James' spot)

<u>STAGE</u> <u>LEFT</u>
  Navy blue Georgetown sweatshirt
  Brown loafers (set at Kendall's spot)
<u>BASIC</u>
  V neck undershirt (2)
  Athletic socks
  White knee pads

<u>ACT</u> I
  Light tan pleated pants
  Med. brown braided belt
  Grey and black striped dress shirt
  Nike hightops
  Blue tie

<u>ACT</u> <u>II</u>
  Taupe pleated pants
  Dark brown braided belt
  Black stripe shirt
  Blue tie (same as in Act I)

BASKETBALL
Adds Trinity sweatshirt from locker on stage

GRADUATION
Adds checked shirt & tie on stage with help of James
Adds Tweed sport coat & Loafers with help of Kendall

CURTAIN
Adds Georgetown Sweatshirt on left; needs assistance

FATHER LARKIN
PRESETS
STAGE LEFT
Priest white/gold/red embroidered animals stole
White linen alb
Chasuble of white with beige/gold edging w/applique
cross CF
Trinity sweatsuit
White tennis shoes
Shoe horn
Black Overcoat

BASIC
Black 2-pc suit
Pewter lapel cross
Black belt
Black socks
Black shoes
Wire rim glasses
White hankie

ACT I
Black Button Shirt
White plastic neck inserts
Large purple priest shawl
In right-hand pocket of coat small purple priest shawl

ACT II
Black shirt with velcro
White plastic inserts

Add on left, Priest Vestments

BASKETBALL
On left, out of Black suit into Trinity sweats & shoes (assist)
GRADUATION
On left, out of sweats, back into Black Suit (assist)

LEE CORTEZ
PRESETS
ON STAGE
Locker #467 Navy blue Georgetown Sweatshirt
Stage Right Balcony on nail—blue sweater

STAGE RIGHT
Blue griffin tee shirt

STAGE LEFT
#2 & #3 Red plaid shirts
White double breasted suit
Python belt

Brown, black & white rayon shirt
White silk tie
Python Nikes
Beige silk hankie in coat pocket
Panama hat

BASIC
Distressed blue jeans
Red longjohn top
Red knee pads
2 pair white athletic socks
Distressed tennis shoes

ACT I
#1 Red plaid shirt
Adds on left #2 red plaid shirt then #3 red plaid shirt
Adds on stage blue sweatshirt & blue sweater

ACT II
Dry red longjohn shirt
#2 Red plaid shirt elbow pad
Adds on left Graduation suit (assist)

CURTAIN
On right adds blue griffin tee shirt. He removes the
bloody shirt, coat & tie, does this change himself.

HENRY RODRIGUEZ
PRESETS
STAGE LEFT
Trinity Sweatshirt

BASIC
  Black socks
  Cross on chain

ACT I
  Black Girbaud pleated pants
  Purple long sleeve top
  Black leather belt with pewter tips
  Black quasi motorcycle boots
  Black leather jacket

ACT II
  Black faded jeans Black tank top
  Nike hightops
  Belt from ACT I

GRADUATION
  Black 2-pc suit
  Rust rayon dress shirt
  Black printed socks
  Black pointed toe shoes with silver buckles

BASKETBALL
  Adds on stage left, Trinity Sweatshirt

BURKE KENDALL
PRESETS
STAGE RIGHT
  Trinity Sweatsuit
  Tennis shoes

STAGE LEFT
2-pc double-breasted grey suit w/ bird lapel pin
Turquoise pocket hankie
Turquoise print silk tie
Grey dress shirt w/ arm insets
Black loafers w/fringe

BASIC
Black flecked wool pants
Grey argyle socks
Black belt
Vest style undershirt
Black loafers

ACT I
Grey dress shirt
Blue/green/white stripe tie
Grey wool sportcoat w/arm patches
Tan/black checked sport coat
Gold/blue striped tie

ACT II
Yellow dress shirt
Navy/white/yellow striped tie
White/grey/black sport coat

BASKETBALL
Put on Stage Right, Trinity sweatsuit & shoes

GRADUATION
Put on Stage Left, needs assistance

MITCHELL JAMES
PRESETS
<u>STAGE RIGHT</u>
 3-pc Khaki suit
 Beige dress shirt
 Mustard silk tie
 Brown lace-up shoes

<u>STAGE LEFT</u>
 Trinity sweatsuit
 Tennis shoes

<u>BASIC</u>
 Beige striped socks
 Watch
 Brown lace-up shoes (note he has two pairs)
 School ring?

<u>ACT I</u>
 Green cord pants
 Beige/white striped shirt
 Green/maroon paisley tie
 Mustard sweater vest
  Brown/beige tweed sport coat w/pocket protector and
assorted pens lapel pins: American Legion, Anti-Abortion,
Red Bird
 Lighter brown canvas belt

<u>ACT 2</u>
 Grey/green plaid pants
 Beige/brown stripe shirt

Mustard/brown silk tie
Green sweater vest
Green/brown/rust plaid sportcoat w/pocket protector and
pens lapel pins: Try Jesus, Mary Save Me
Darker brown canvas belt

BASKETBALL
Put on Stage Left (assist)

GRADUATION
Put on Stage Right

MARCO
PRESETS
STAGE RIGHT
Trinity sweatsuit
Grey/brown checked seersucker pants
Black/brown paisley belt
Mustard shirt
Orange silk tie w/angel tie tack
Brown raw silk sport coat w/purple striped pocket hankie
lapel pin; graduation
Gold/purple socks
Black/brown spectator shoes

STAGE LEFT
Big Black RAP Coat (gets pre set on stage at
intermission)

BASIC
Faded blue jeans

White athletic socks
Reebok pump high tops

ACT I
Green tee shirt
NYC orange distressed sweatshirt

ACT II
Green tank top
Green/brown/orange painted long sleeve shirt

BASKETBALL
Put on Stage right

GRADUATION
Put on Stage Right

FREDDIE
PRESETS
STAGE RIGHT
Trinity sweatsuit

STAGE LEFT (if dressing room is close by he can go there)
Grey pants
Black belt
Black shirt w/purple tips
Green sport coat w/angel wings on lapel
Green/lavender jagged pattern silk pocket hankie
Black/purple socks
Black shoes w/silver tips

<u>BASIC</u>
Faded grey jeans w/doodle
White athletic socks
Cotton grey duck vest w/assorted patches
Red/white high top Nikes

<u>ACT I</u>
Yellow/black striped shirt
Gold/green long sleeved knit shirt

<u>ACT II</u>
Gold tee shirt
Black/gold heavy striped shirt

<u>BASKETBALL</u>
Puts on stage right

<u>GRADUATION</u>
Puts on in his room if it is SL and close by

CARLOS
PRESETS
<u>STAGE RIGHT</u>
Trinity sweatsuit
Brown striped pants
Orange shirt
Black tie w/crosses and rosary
Brown sport coat w/striped lapels, Honor pin
Grey belt
Black/brown fur look shoes

BASIC
Green/Black/magenta cotton striped pants
Black belt w/turquoise stone buckle
Brown socks
Distressed brown leather vest
Black/green checked bicycle cap
Black high tops

ACT I
Purple/green striped long sleeve tee shirt
Purple tee shirt w/orange neck

ACT II
Purple tank top
Blue/green/purple tie dyed shirt

BASKETBALL
Puts on Stage right

GRADUATION
Puts on Stage right

PROPERTY PLOT:

I,1:
Gun for shots (offstage)
Large purple liturgical stole
Liturgical pail with water and sprinkler

I,2:
Two benches (all purpose for all scenes)
Eight lockers
Chalk board
Chalk
Eraser
Paper for Lee's "doodle"

I,4:
Papers and markbooks for teachers
Chalkboard
Chalk
Text book for Griffin

I,5:
Stool
Twenty dollar bill

I,6:
Pocket notebook for Larkin
Mechanical pencil
Text books for Griffin
Sports jacket for Griffin
5 comics
Drawing of the Baron

Basketball

I,7:
Markbooks and papers for teachers
Pocket flask with tea
2 paper cups

I,8:
Two large boxes of comics

I,9:
Large purple stole for Larkin
Change of shirt for Lee
Liturgical bells for mass
Basketball

I,10:
Small purple stole (from Larkin's pocket)
I,ll:
Leather artist's portfolio
Three packages wrapped for Christmas
One wrapped package of tapes (to be smashed)
Winter jackets for Griffin and Lee
Drawing of the Griffin (done on flash paper)
Lighter

II,3:
A dollar bill

II,4:
Basketball

II,5 :
Fight bell

II,6:
Markbooks for teachers

II,7:
Chalk board
Chalk

II,8:
Basketball
Henry's backpack

II,9:
Artist's portfolio filled with vandalized drawings

II,10:
Referee whistles
Basketball
Camera with working flash
Complete change of clothes (formal) for Griffin's onstage
    change -II,11:
Gun for shots (offstage)

II,12:
Large purple stole
Liturgical pail, water, sprinkler
Chalk to outline Lee's body (Kendall)
Blood pack

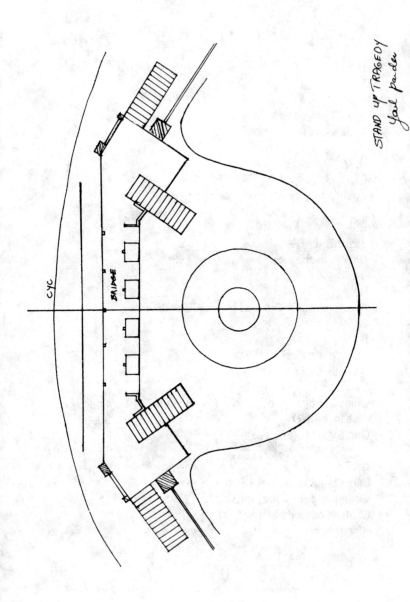

CYC

BRIDGE

STAND UP TRAGEDY
Paul Pander

Other Publications for Your Interest

A MAP OF THE WORLD
(ADVANCED GROUPS—DRAMA)
By DAVID HARE

7 men, 4 women, plus extras—2 Interiors

This new play by the author of *Plenty* "is an ambitious work which brings together in heated discussion a young left wing journalist and a right wing expatriate Indian novelist. The settings are a Bombay hotel where they are attending a world poverty conference and the British film studio where the Indian author's experiences are being turned into a film. Throughout the play, life and fiction overlap . . . One of the issues is the sexual jealousy that arises over the men's competition for the favours of a promiscuous American actress staying at the hotel. Also on the agenda: idealism vs. cynicism; the West's arrogance in its handling of Third World problems; the alleged evils of Zionism; and the journalist's fervent belief in the necessity for change."—London Sunday Express. "It is a pleasure to hear a stage echoing to such issues and such talk."—London Standard. "A rich and complex play built around a series of antitheses: the Third World and the West, fiction and reality, irony and committment, reason and passion, the personal and the political. Yet for me what makes it the most mature and moving of Hare's works to date is its gut conviction that once we lose our Utopian dreams we have lost everything."—London Guardian.   (#15620)

NANAWATAI
(ADVANCED GROUPS—DRAMA)
By WILLIAM MASTROSIMONE

10 men, 1 woman, plus chorus of female extras—Unit set

The intrepid Mr. Mastrosimone, heretofore the author of studies of character such as *The Woolgatherer*, *A Tantalizing*, *Shivaree* and *Extremities*, has here set his sights on an epic scale. Shortly after the Soviet Union invaded Afghanistan, Mr. Mastrosimone managed to get himself smuggled into that beleaguered country via Pakistan. There he spent several weeks with the Afghani rebels, observing their often futile attempts to resist the Russian blitzkrieg. All of the resistance he witnessed was not futile, though; he also observed the capture and execution of a Soviet tank crew. It was this incident which inspired *Nanawatai* (an Afghani word which means "sanctuary"). The story is told through the dual points of view of a Russian tank crew member and an Afghani rebel, as a chorus of village women impresses upon us the effect on the citizenry of all the bloodshed (not unlike, of course, in a Greek tragedy). "Hard-hitting and probing . . . alive with issues and conflicts of both a political and personal nature."—Hollywood Reporter. "It has the ritual power of Greek tragedy."—L.A. Times.   (#15975)

Other Publications for Your Interest

OTHER PEOPLE'S MONEY
(LITTLE THEATRE—DRAMA)

By JERRY STERNER

3 men, 2 women—One Set

Wall Street takeover artist Lawrence Garfinkle's intrepid computer is going "tilt" over the undervalued stock of New England Wire & Cable. He goes after the vulnerable company, buying up its stock to try and take over the company at the annual meeting. If the stockholders back Garfinkle, they will make a bundle—but what of the 1200 employees? What of the local community? Too bad, says Garfinkle, who would then liquidate the company—take the money and run. Set against the charmingly rapacious financier are Jorgenson, who has run the company since the Year One and his chief operations officer, Coles, who understands, unlike the genial Jorgenson, what a threat Garfinkle poses to the firm. They bring in Kate, a bright young woman lawyer, who specializes in fending off takeovers—and who is the daughter of Jorgenson's administrative assistant, Bea. Kate must not only contend with Garfinkle—she must also move Jorgenson into taking decisive action. Should they use "greenmail"? Try to find a "White Knight"? Employ a "shark repellent"? This compelling drama about Main Street vs. Wall Street is as topical and fresh as today's headlines, giving its audience an inside look at what's *really going on* in this country and asking trenchant questions, not the least of which is whether a corporate raider is really the creature from the Black Lagoon of capitalism or the Ultimate Realist come to save business from itself.

(#17064)

THE DOWNSIDE
(LITTLE THEATRE—COMEDY)

By RICHARD DRESSER

6 men, 2 women—Combination Interior

These days, American business is a prime target for satire, and no recent play has cut as deep, with more hilarious results, than this superb new comedy from the Long Wharf Theatre, Mark & Maxwell, a New Jersey pharmaceuticals firm, has acquired U.S. rights to market an anti-stress drug manufactured in Europe, pending F.D.A. approval; but the marketing executives have got to come up with a snazzy ad campaign by January—and here we are in December! The irony is that nowhere is this drug more needed than right there at Mark & Maxwell, a textbook example of corporate ineptitude, where it seems all you have to do to get ahead is look good in a suit. The marketing strategy meetings get more and more pointless and frenetic as the deadline approaches. These meetings are "chaired" by Dave, the boss, who is never actually there—he is a voice coming out of a box, as Dave phones in while jetting to one meeting or another, eventually directing the ad campaign on his mobile phone while his plane is being hijacked! Doesn't matter to Dave, though—what matters is the possible "downside" of this new drug: hallucinations. "Ridiculous", says the senior marketing executive Alan: who then proceeds to tell how Richard Nixon comes to his house in the middle of the night to visit . . . "Richard Dresser's deft satirical sword pinks the corporate image repeatedly, leaving the audience amused but thoughtful."—Meriden Record. "Funny and ruthlessly cynical."—Phila. Inquirer. "A new comedy that is sheer delight."—Westport News. "The Long Wharf audience laughed a lot, particularly those with office training. But they were also given something to ponder about the way we get things done in America these days, or rather pretend to get things done. No wonder the Japanese are winning."—L.A. Times.

(#6718)

Other Publications for Your Interest

DOMINO
(ADVANCED GROUPS—COMIC DRAMA)
By ROBERT LITZ

6 men, 1 woman to play various roles/Unit Set.

This "excruciatingly funny political comedy" (N.Y. Post) is about a rather thick U.S. foreign loan banker who visits a Central American banana republic, supervised by a charmingly cynical C.I.A. operative, to renegotiate a 3.8 billion dollar debt. Unwittingly, he winds up financing and masterminding the overthrow of the government. Written in short, hilarious scenes (well, "hilarious" in a rather frightening way...) *Domino* has a lot to tell us about what what is really going on in these days of Contras, Sandinistas and Noriegas. "Hostages are taken; prisoners are tortured; ransoms are paid; weapons are hijacked; drugs are traded; political deals are struck—and press conferences are held to celebrate the whole sordid mess. Then, when the C.I.A. discovers a more expedient way to sell off the country to capitalist interests, everybody betrays everybody else, and the whole cycle is played all over again. After a while you can't tell the corrupt generals from the bought-out guerillas. And if there ever was a hero, or an honest idealist, in the house, somebody shot him."—N.Y. Post. $4.00

(#6165)

EL SALVADOR
(LITTLE THEATRE—DRAMA)
By RAFAEL LIMA

6 men, 1 woman—Interior.

This brilliant new naturalistic drama from NYC's famed Circle Repertory takes place in a hotel room in El Salvador which has been converted into a home base for a dissolute and mostly disillusioned gaggle of U.S. TV journalists, fed up with the futility of constantly risking their lives reporting on a revolution that nobody back home cares about. Not that *they* care much, either—but it does give them something to talk about. The play takes place on a day when the El Salvador military, flying sophisticated helicopters provided them by the U.S. government, have bombed a small remote village, killing many civilians, including women and children. That night, as they wait out an attack on the capital and, possibly, on the hotel, the crew members talk of their feelings about the war, their shame about America's role in it, and their separation from loved ones far away. "A tensely fascinating evening in the theatre."—N.Y. Post. "*The Front Page* transposed to a Third World war zone."—Village Voice. "A powerful, gripping drama...has the ring of authenticity that is as vivid as reality. You are absolutely there."—UPI. "Lima knows his subject and has illuminated it with pungent dialogue and crackling theatricalism."—N.Y. Daily News.

(#7024)

Other Publications for Your Interest

SPOILS OF WAR
(LITTLE THEATRE—DRAMA)
By MICHAEL WELLER

3 men, 3 women—Various Interior settings

Heretofore best known as the author of trenchant, bittersweet comedies such as *Loose Ends* and *Moonchildren*, as well as the screenplays for *Hair* and *Ragtime*, Mr. Weller is here in a deeper, more somber mode, as he chronicles the desperate attempts of a sixteen year-old boy to reconcile his divorced parents. Nobody writes better about disillusionment, about people whose hopes and dreams never quite lived up to reality. In *Moonchildren* and *Loose Ends* Mr. Weller dealt with how the Dream ended up in the sixties and seventies, respectively; here, the fuzzy decade of the fifties is explored through the eyes of Martin's parents, ex-thirties radicals who have chosen very different ways to cope with the changed, changing times. Elyse, the mother, is still a bohemian, a rebel without a cause who wants to live for something more than the rent and the price of hamburger, whereas Andrew, the father, has dropped back into the system, and accepted Life As It Is. And Martin is caught between these finally irreconcilable outlooks, unable to bring his parents back together and wondering what path *his* life will take. "Mr. Weller finds in one family's distintegration a paradigm of the postwar collapse of liberal idealism. This is without question Mr. Weller's most intelligent play, always intelligent and at times moving."—N.Y. Times. "Emotionally charged...a touching, lovely work."—N.Y. Post.
(#21294)

SPEED-THE-PLOW
(ADVANCED GROUPS—SERIOUS COMEDY)
By DAVID MAMET

2 men, 1 woman—Two interior. (may be simply suggested).

This is, without a doubt one of Mamet's best plays (including *American Buffalo* and the stunning, Pulitzer Prize-winning *Glengarry Glen Ross*). Joe Mantegna, Ron Silver and Madonna starred on Broadway in this hilarious and devastating satire of Hollywood, a microcosm of the macrocosm of American culture. Charlie Fox has discovered a terrific vehicle for a certain "hot" male movie star, and has brought it to his "best friend" Bobby Gould, "Head of Production" for a major film company. He coulda taken it across the street; but no, he's brought it to Bobby. Both see the script as their ticket to the really big table, where the real power is. The star wants to do it, and all they have to do is "pitch" it to their boss. The screenplay is a mass of typical action-picture cliches, which they have decided to pitch as a "buddy film"—the current "hot commodity". They'll be taking a meeting with the studio boss tomorrow; but tonight, Bobby has bet Charlie $500 that he can seduce Karen, a temp secretary. His ruse: he has given her a novel "by some Eastern sissy writer" which he has been asked to "courtesy-read" before saying thanks-but-no-thanks. Karen reads the novel and comes to Bobby's house that night—to convince him that *this*, and *not* the buddy film, should be the company's next project. Her arguments are convincing—all the more so when she agrees to sleep with Bobby, an experience which is apparently so transmogrifying that, much to Charlie's surprise, the next morning he finds he has to plead with Bobby not to put the buddy film "in turnaround", not to pitch the gloomy "sissy film". "By turns hilarious and chilling...[the] dialogue skyrockets."—N.Y. Times. Mamet's clearest, wittiest play."—N.Y. Daily News. "I laughed and laughed. The play is crammed with wonderful, dazzling, brilliant lines."—N.Y. Post. "There isn't a line that isn't somehow insanely funny or scarily insane."—Newsweek.
(#21281)